The Manager as Mentor

**Recent Titles in
The Manager as...**

The Manager as Politician
Jerry W. Gilley

The Manager as Change Leader
Ann Gilley

The Manager as Mentor

Michael J. Marquardt and Peter Loan

The Manager as. . .
Jerry W. Gilley, Series Editor

Westport, Connecticut
London

HD
38.15
.M38
2006

Library of Congress Cataloging-in-Publication Data

Marquardt, Michael J.
    The manager as mentor / Michael J. Marquardt and Peter Loan.
        p. cm. — (The manager as ..., ISSN 1555-7480)
    Includes bibliographical references and index.
    ISBN 0-275-98589-X
    1. Management—Handbooks, manuals, etc. 2. Mentoring. I. Loan, Peter.
II. Title. III. Series.
    HD38.15.M38   2006
    658.3′124—dc22   2005020583

British Library Cataloguing in Publication Data is available.

Library of Congress Catalog Card Number: 2005020583
ISBN: 0-275-98589-X
ISSN: 1555-7480

First published in 2006

Praeger Publishers, 88 Post Road West, Westport, CT 06881
An imprint of Greenwood Publishing Group, Inc.
www.praeger.com

Printed in the United States of America

The paper used in this book complies with the
Permanent Paper Standard issued by the National
Information Standards Organization (Z39.48-1984).

10 9 8 7 6 5 4 3 2 1

Contents

PART II
Action Plan, Tools, and Resources

Publisher's Note

The backbone of every organization, large or small, is its managers. They guide and direct employees' actions, decisions, resources, and energies. They serve as friends and leaders, motivators and disciplinarians, problem solvers and counselors, partners and directors. Managers serve as liaisons between executives and employees, interpreting the organization's mission and realizing its goals. They are responsible for performance improvement, quality, productivity, strategy, *and* execution—through the people who work for and with them. All too often, though, managers are thrust into these roles and responsibilities without adequate guidance and support. MBA programs provide book learning but little practical experience in the art of managing projects and people; at the other end of the spectrum, exceptional talent in one's functional area does not necessarily prepare the individual for the daily rigors of supervision. This series is designed to address those gaps directly.

The Manager as … series provides a unique library of insights and information designed to help managers develop a portfolio of outstanding skills. From Mentor to Marketer, Politician to Problem Solver, Coach to Change Leader, each book provides an introduction to the principles, concepts, and issues that define the role; discusses the evolution of recent and current trends; and guides the reader through the dynamic process of assessing their strengths and weaknesses and creating a personal development plan. Featuring diagnostic tools, exercises, checklists, case examples, practical tips, and recommended resources, the books in this series will help readers at any stage in their careers master the art and science of management.

PART I

Principles and Practices

ONE

Mentoring for Corporate Success

Probably the most important and valuable role a manager can perform in today's rapidly changing environment is to mentor and inspire the people around him or her to learn. By nurturing talent, inspiring individual development, and facilitating excellence, a manager's mentoring can enhance the organization's probability for global success. Mentoring is not an easy competency to develop, much less master. Many managers, who may be great at leading or coaching others and coordinating projects and programs, may be disasters as mentors. As a result, opportunities for individual and organizational effectiveness are lost.

THE IMPORTANCE OF MENTORING

Mentoring is an age-old practice whose name traces in Greek mythology to Odysseus's friend, Mentor, whom he entrusted as guide to the development of his son, Telemachus. Over the years, mentoring has played an important role in the development of individuals and organizations worldwide.

Today, however, the manner and importance of mentoring has begun to change, and it is influenced by new forms of work, technology, and learning. Mentoring is sweeping through corporate America and is attracting attention in government and nonprofit sectors as well. Mentoring typically has been defined as a relationship between an experienced person and a less experienced person in which the mentor provides guidance, advice, support, and feedback to the mentee. Mentoring helps new employees learn about organizational culture and facilitate personal and career growth and development.

The old model of informal relationships that provided ambitious employees ways to achieve their career goals has given way to a diversity of learning-focused mentoring programs that are helping build the next generation of leaders.[1] Mentoring has also expanded opportunities for those who traditionally have faced societal and organizational barriers to career growth, such as women and minorities. The benefits of mentoring have begun to extend beyond the workplace to expand cultural awareness and enhance the potential for meaningful lives.[2]

The diversity of mentoring environments has generated a number of working definitions of mentoring. Mentoring can be:

- a one-to-one, nonjudgmental relationship in which an individual voluntarily gives time to support and encourage another. This is typically developed at a time of transition in the mentee's life and lasts for a significant and sustained period of time;
- support, assistance, advocacy, or guidance given by one person to another in order to achieve an objective or several objectives over a period of time;
- an adult who can provide a pupil with the benefit of his or her life, school, or work experience with a view to encouraging the pupil to move confidently through a range of new experiences;
- off-line help by one person to another in making significant transitions in knowledge, work, or thinking;
- the support of one individual by another within a personal relationship developed through regular contact over a period of time;
- a process by which an older and more experienced person takes a younger person under his or her wing, freely offering advice, support, and encouragement. The older person (the mentor) becomes, among other things, a role model who inspires the younger person (the mentee).[3]

James Freedman, president of the American Academy of Arts and Sciences had two mentors in his life—the first, Alexander Bickel, his law professor at Yale, and the second, Thurgood Marshall, for whom Freedman was a law clerk. Freedman recalls the importance of each.

"Alex Bickel had an enormous impact on me. He is a man who was born in Bucharest, came to this country at age twelve, became a brilliant student himself, and clerked for Justice Frankfurter. He was, in the classroom, electric. Alex Bickel had a mind of enormous originality. He encouraged students to engage him and debate him. He was enormously generous. He helped me when I wanted to enter law teaching. Alex Bickel was the most important teacher I've ever had."

Thurgood Marshall "was so different from my law school professors, who were, of course, very scholarly and intellectual. I went to work for him right out of law school. He was a practical man. He wanted to know how trials worked, and when errors were made, allegedly, in lower courts. He was looking at trial tactics; he was looking at why they occurred. He was a much more pragmatic man than most law professors were, and that added a very nice dimension to my own growth....He was a person who had a sense of destiny, and you could just feel it. Occasionally, you meet such individuals among your friends. You occasionally see such qualities in students. Thurgood Marshall knew from a very young age that he was destined to do important things. He felt it. He believed it. He wanted it. And he did have a heroic mind. It is interesting to me that once Brown against the Board was decided, he had really achieved his destiny. And that's when he began to think of other things. And, of course, finally became a judge."[4]

As there are various perspectives on mentoring, there are various notions, as well, regarding mentors. Mentors may be:

- people who, through their actions and work, help others to achieve their potential;
- someone who helps another person, usually younger, on a one-to-one basis through an important transition;
- many things—a positive role model, an adviser, an experienced friend. Somebody from outside a person's immediate circle taking a special interest can make an enormous difference.

Within the variety of mentoring situations and settings is a generic core support that is given voluntarily by one person to another. What makes mentoring unique includes:

- its objectives—what it hopes to achieve;
- the mentor pairing—combinations of young person and adult, matches as peers, colleagues, or by gender, cultural background, and career objectives;
- the intensity and time commitment given to the mentoring relationship;
- the amount and the content of mentor preparation and training.

Because mentoring takes place in many forms and with many groups, it can mean different things to different people. Mentoring can span a continuum from coaching and tutoring, to a holistic, whole-person approach, involving a high degree of personal commitment. According to Clutterbuck, there are two major schools of mentoring.[5]

1. **The Traditional School:** This originated in the United States and involves sponsorship, hands-on help, tapping into the authority and contacts of the senior partner, and focuses mostly on career development through mentee-focused learning.
2. **The Developmental School:** This originated in Europe and focuses on a two-way learning partnership and expects that the mentee will do more for himself or herself. Here the focus is on developing the mentee's capabilities.

The realization that everyone does not have the same understanding of the mentoring process is particularly important for multinational companies that introduce mentoring as part of the employee development process.

Over dinner, Wayne, a bureau chief with a large federal agency, shares with his wife, Wendy, an office director at an aerospace corporation, that he has been asked to "volunteer" to be a mentor.

"I'm already overworked, and I'm not sure I have the skills to be a mentor, even with the training I will get."

"Wayne, you are very insightful, and you do listen well when you make the effort. Mentoring has worked well for me, and I think you will be an effective mentor."

"But your situation is different, Wendy. First, you have the soft skills, and in your corporate environment people want to improve their skills and advance. Where I am, most people feel entitled to their jobs and don't put out extra effort."

"Well," Wendy replied, "you really should think about it. Both government and the private sector have been eliminating middle management positions, and those of us who are left feel overworked. Mentoring can empower others to step up and take more responsibility. Maybe the investment you make will eventually decrease your workload."

"Hmm, maybe so; I'll give it some thought," replied Wayne.

THE REVIVAL OF MENTORING

Two broad currents have reintroduced and reaffirmed the value of mentoring in the modern workplace. One is the centrality of learning to the long-term development of individuals and teams for corporate success; the second concerns the rapid changes in the world of work.

Importance of Learning to Long-Term Development of Individuals and Teams for Corporate Success

In this age of knowledge the long-term development of individuals is essential for the success of companies, government agencies, nonprofit organizations, indeed, for healthy civic life. Organizational growth is directly linked to individual learning and development. People must continue to learn after they complete their college experiences. Increasingly, it is not the formal knowledge that one learns in college, graduate school, or business school that is valuable to companies, but the learning that comes from being open to all sorts of stimuli and the disposition to craft relationships from seemingly disparate information.

In such times as these, the questions for organizations are how to manage knowledge and how to keep all employees in a frame of constant learning.

When Robert H. Buckman, chairman of the board for Bulab Holdings, the parent company of Buckman Laboratories, addressed the International Association of Business Communicators conference in Washington, D.C., in 2000, he said his company must share knowledge to increase the speed of innovation and meet the changing needs of customers and increase the global speed of response. The flexible and mobile organization relies on the faster growth of talented people who flourish in a climate of continuity and trust.[6]

A company's growth is directly linked with employee development. More and more companies are turning to training programs to harness a corporate culture capable of being more innovative and flexible.[7]

Yet even traditional training programs must be scrutinized. Much traditional training engages in, as McElroy notes, "something we endure in response to other people's views on what they think we should know."[8]

As knowledge is created daily and as people must continue to learn after they leave formal college and university training, organizations must identify ongoing learning opportunities for employees at all levels. Many organizations have accepted that they must become learning organizations and have adopted a host of powerful tools to promote workplace learning, problem solving, and quality improvement; programs include action learning, Six Sigma, and human performance improvement (HPI). As the importance of collaboration, respect for the person, and employee retention have become recognized, an age-old learning tool has been revived and adapted to the needs of today's organizations. Mentoring is a growing phenomenon in organizations, and managers are increasingly taking responsibility for the mentoring of employees.

Today, people in organizations are becoming increasingly aware that the knowledge, the strategies, the leadership, and the technology of yesterday will not lead to success in tomorrow's world. Companies must increase their corporate capacity to learn if they are to function successfully in an environment that includes continual mergers, rapid technological changes, massive societal change, and increasing competition. These challenges and the potential benefits to organizations virtually assured the emergence of a new species of learning organization.

Companies have come to realize that to obtain and sustain competitive advantage in this new world, they must evolve to a higher form of learning capability and to learn better and faster from their successes and failures, from within and from without. They must transform themselves into organizations in which everyone, groups and individuals, increases their adaptive and productive capabilities. Without increasing their capacity to learn, they will not avoid the fate of the dinosaur, unable to adapt to its changing environment.

In pursuit of better deployment of human capital, learning speeds new workers' readiness to do the new job and fit the role needed. We now have a new metric, "time to competence." Learning is the foundation of professional development, the ongoing growth of human capital from which companies derive more innovation, higher levels of service, and greater margins. Learning is the key to adapting and surviving massive discontinuities in markets and competitive environments. It is the shock absorber for the speed bumps of change.

Mentoring is a process of engagement and learning is its fundamental purpose. Mentoring is most successful when learning needs determine its structure, when it is done collaboratively, and when commitment to learning by the mentoring partners is its key element.

Both the mentor and mentee embark upon a learning journey. Their respective and parallel learning is based in their relationship and enables them to challenge, support, and articulate their vision.

As Zachary notes, the new mentor/mentee paradigm has the mentor as facilitator and guide of the learning process ("sage on the stage, to guide on the side").[9] The mentee is not fed wisdom at the feet of the mentor, but he or she discovers it in relationship to the mentor and both learn.

A famous mentor-mentee pairing is found in the relationship between Thomas Jefferson and Meriwether Lewis. *The Journals of Lewis and Clark* chronicle the guidance and support provided by Jefferson to prepare Lewis for shepherding the journey westward across America. These two men shared in the moment-to-moment planning and preparation for the exploration and scientific discovery of the uncharted western territories.[10]

Rapid Changes in the World of Work

Sweeping changes have occurred in workplace relationships between workers, their mangers, and their organizations. These changes include: (1) technology, (2) globalization, (3) changes in the workplace, (4) restructuring of companies into learning organizations, (5) growing importance of knowledge, (6) changing roles and expectations of workers, (7) innovation, and (8) the merging of leadership and management.

Technology. The impact of technology on organizations, management, and learning is turning the world of work on its head. Some organizations are becoming more virtual than physical because of technology. People may spend more time with customers in Kuala Lumpur than with coworkers across the hall. Technology has caused learning to become the prime purpose of business, and learning, as Zuboff proclaims, has become "the new form of labor."[11]

Technology increasingly requires that managers manage knowledge rather than manage people. Technology alters the *how* and *why* workers learn. Employees now need to train themselves via self-directed learning. And workplace learning no longer assumes a fixed time and location with a group of people for just-in-case purposes; instead, it is being implemented on a just-what's-needed, just-in-time, and just-where-it's-needed basis. The technological forces that have already restructured work will force those who are responsible for employee development to "create ever more flexible and responsive learning and performance solutions."[12]

Globalization and Diversity. Although images of autoworkers lining up to punch their time cards linger with those of us who still have a nostalgic foot in the Industrial Age, our changing global economy is better represented today by images of people coming and going at all hours, dressed in ties, tank tops, and turbans, working at home, at telecenters, or on the road, forming ad hoc teams, and collaborating across continents.

The global economy has created global organizations, companies that operate as if the entire world were a single entity. They are so fully integrated that all their activities link, leverage, and compete on a worldwide scale. Global firms emphasize global operations over national or multinational operations. They use global sourcing of human resources, capital, technology, facilities, resources, and raw materials. They deem cultural sensitivity to employees, customers, and patterns as critical to the success of the organization. Globalization of an organization has occurred when the organization has developed a global corporate culture, strategy, and structure as well as global operations and global people.[13]

Success depends upon the ability of the organization to compete globally for every industry and sector throughout the world. Even the largest companies in the biggest markets will not be able to survive based on their domestic markets alone. Thinking and operating globally will be critical to organizational survival and growth in the twenty-first century.

The growing similarity of what customers wish to purchase, including quality and price, has spurred both opportunities and pressures for businesses to become global. More and more companies, whether small or large, young or old, recognize that they must become global or become extinct.

Institutes of management education are recognizing that in a pluralistic world new approaches to managing across cultures should begin long before one enters the workforce. The recent proliferation of international executive MBA programs highlights the need for managers who can function in different cultures. Recently, for example, the Asian Academy of Management was established at the Chinese University in Hong Kong because of the dissatisfaction among both academics and managers in Asia that Western models of management are inadequate in Asian cultures.[14]

In multicultural environments, managers must develop or enhance skills such as:

- active listening;
- becoming aware of one's own assumptions and worldviews;
- understanding the beliefs and values systems of other cultures;
- developing relationships with people from other cultures; and
- adopting the appropriate communication strategy in negotiation and conflict resolution.[15]

Until recently, it was normal for global corporations to be headed by nationals of the mother company. Today it is becoming a common arrangement to have local executives take the rein of foreign companies, even as expatriates continue to staff the senior management ranks. Among global corporations, both Nestle-Philippines and Procter & Gamble-Philippines, two of the country's largest foreign corporations have Filipino CEOs. Other global corporations based in the Philippines that now have Filipino chief executives include Shell Petroleum Corporation, Caltex, Amway, IBM, ING Barings, and Coca-Cola Bottlers.[16] Toyota Motor Corporation has appointed non-Japanese citizens as executive chairman of Toyota Motor Corp. Australia Ltd. and as chief operating officer of Toyota Motor Marketing Europe.

Changes in the Workplace.   Both the world of work and the world of the workplace have been transformed. Many workers no longer work in an office. Corporations collaborate and compete with one another at the same time. Customers provide supervision as well as dictate services. Fellow employees work closely with one another though never meet. Companies have temporary, part-time CEOs and permanent full-time janitors. Corporate headquarters staff may consist of less than 1 percent of the company's workforce, if there is a headquarters.

> "The biggest challenge is not having those hallway conversations, especially when you're moving as fast as we are," concedes Frank Ianna, president of AT&T Network Services, based in Basking Ridge, New Jersey. "We use communications and information technology to work together, whether someone is two floors away or 2,000 miles away," he points out. "Remote communication is a given today. If you can't manage and work remotely, you're not going to be successful."[17]

Organizations have moved from the quality efforts of the 1980s through the reengineering processes of the 1990s to the radical transformation of the workplace itself as we enter the twenty-first century. Focuses on the reduction of defects and the streamlining of business processes have been superseded by a new focus on enabling organizations to manage continuous, white-water change. Companies create high performance work organizations in which work is reorganized, redesigned, and reengineered to improve performance.

Decades of breaking work into ever smaller tasks are coming to an end. Now teams of employees are responsible for key business processes from beginning to end. Impatience with the rate of change causes many organizations to reengineer (start from scratch) their key processes. Virtual organizations are appearing, which build on a few core competencies and assign their other work to temporary and contract workers as needed.

Advances in information technology described previously are providing greater computer power, faster transmission of data, expanded storage capacity, and clearer, more complex links among users. This innovation permits greater control of a more decentralized organization and facilitates the information flow needed to give local managers substantive decision-making authority.

Because of this technology, corporations will become cluster organizations or adhocracies, groups of geographically dispersed people—typically working at home—that come together electronically for a particular project and then disband, having completed their work. More organizations will comprise a minimal core of permanent employees supported by independently contracted professionals.

As more companies realize that the key resources of business are not capital, personnel, or facilities, but rather knowledge, information, and ideas, many new ways of viewing the organization begin to emerge. Everywhere companies are restructuring, creating integrated organizations, global networks, and leaner corporate centers. Organizations are becoming more fluid, ever shifting in size, shape, and arrangements.

Companies organize around what they do best. They structure themselves according to core competencies instead of according to product or market. The organizational architecture of companies evolves around autonomous work teams and strategic alliances.

Companies also coevolve by working with direct competitors, customers, and suppliers to create new businesses, markets, and industries. Soon companies will view themselves as part of a wider environment, a business ecosystem, and will see business opportunities not simply from the perspective of solo players but as players coevolving with many others in relationships of codependency.

Coevolution is sharply different from the conventional idea of competition, in which companies work only with their own resources and do not extend themselves using the capabilities of others. In the global market, companies must rely on other players for capacity, innovation, and capital.

Business Week states that networked (virtual) companies "could become the most important organizational innovation since the 1920s. That was when Pierre DuPont and Alfred Sloan developed the principle of decentralization to organize giant complex corporations."[18] The virtual corporation will have neither central office nor organization chart; it will have no hierarchy or vertical integration. Teams of people in different companies will routinely work together. After the business is done, the network will disband.

The emergence of these network-type organizations replacing the more traditional bureaucratic structures can be summarized by the transformative organizational shifts shown in Table 1.1.

Table 1.1
Organizational Transformation

Dimension	Old	New
Critical tasks	Physical	Mental
Relationships	Hierarchical	Peer-to-peer
Levels	Many	Few
Structures	Functional	Multidisciplinary teams
Boundaries	Fixed	Permeable
Competitive thrust	Vertical integration	Outsourcing and alliances
Management style	Autocratic	Participative
Culture	Compliance	Commitment and results
People	Homogeneous	Diverse
Strategic focus	Efficiency	Innovation

Emergence of Learning Organizations. Over the past 10 years, numerous economic, social, and technological forces have significantly increased in their intensity and dramatically altered the environment of the world of work. These changes have occurred so rapidly and competition has increased so intensely that the large dinosaur organizations with the small pea-sized brains that flourished in the twentieth century cannot breathe and survive in this new atmosphere of the twenty-first century. The survival of the fittest is quickly becoming the survival of the *fittest to learn.*

In his book, *Riding the Tiger: Doing Business in a Transforming World,* Harrison Owen writes, "There was a time when the prime business of business was to make a profit and a product. There is now a prior, prime business, which is to become an effective learning organization. Not that profit and product are no longer important, but without continual learning, profits and products will no longer be possible."[19] Unless an organization continuously adapts to its environment via speedy, effective learning, it will die. In short, external change forces organizations to either adapt or become extinct.

Only organizations that can transform themselves into more intelligent, proficient engines of change will succeed in the new millennium. As Reginald Revans, a pioneer of organizational learning notes, "Learning inside must be equal to or greater than change occurring outside the organization or the organization dies."[20]

The new organizations that emerge will need to possess greater knowledge, flexibility, speed, power, and learning ability so as to better confront the shifting needs of a new environment, of more demanding customers, and of smarter knowledge workers.

The results of successful adaptation are obvious. Organizations that learn faster will achieve significant strategic advantages in the global world of business. The new "learning organization" will be able to harness the collective genius of its people at the individual, group, and system levels. This capability, combined with improved organizational status, technology, knowledge management, and people empowerment, will empower organizations to "blow the competition away."

The Ascendance of Knowledge.   As the twenty-first century opens, the ground seems to shift under our feet. As if a harbinger of things to come, the Y-2K crisis instilled in us a fear of organizational disaster if we were to lose touch with our information bases. Yet this fear was quickly overwhelmed by the global realization that new knowledge, created daily, can overwhelm organizations that are not prepared for the changing requirements of management in the age of knowledge. The basic competitive elements of the past were material, capital, and the capability for mass production. Today, information, knowledge, and creativity are emerging as the sine qua non of competitive elements.

In the knowledge age, the sharing of knowledge is the means to gaining power and success. Hoarding and withholding of knowledge are the hallmarks of an earlier time. When knowledge is recognized as an unlimited resource, however, one that may be created continuously, then employees and managers alike become collaborators in producing and sharing it.

Sharing knowledge is not about giving people something or getting something from them. That is only valid for information sharing. Sharing knowledge occurs when people are genuinely interested in helping one another develop new capacities for action; it is about creating learning processes. The knowledge age is forcing new organizational structures that are less hierarchical, more flexible, and more dependent on the creative process of all employees.

New knowledge changes us. It challenges our assumptions, forces us to rethink our previous conclusions and solutions, forces us out of our cultural niches, and makes us humble in the face of the unknown. To manage the constant flow of new knowledge, organizations must manage this change process. As Drucker puts it:

> …in a period of upheaval, such as the one we are living in, change is the norm. To be sure, it is painful and risky, and above all, it requires a great deal of very hard work. But unless an organization sees that its task is to *lead* change, that organization—whether a business, a university, or a hospital—will not survive. In a period of rapid structural change the only organizations that survive are the "change leaders." It is therefore

a central 21st-century challenge for management that its organization becomes a change leader.[21]

The wealth of nations will depend increasingly on knowledge-based, high-tech industries in areas such as biotechnology, health, environmental products and services, tourism and hospitality, telecommunications, computer software and software applications, financial services, and entertainment (film, television, games). These are all highly competitive global industries. Keeping even a few months ahead of the competition, in terms of innovation and knowledge, is critical to survival.

Information—processed by human brain work into knowledge, integrated and intuited into wisdom—has quite suddenly become the world's most important resource. Knowledge will be playing the prima donna role in world history that physical labor, minerals, and energy once played.

Simply put, knowledge has become more important for organizations than financial resources, market position, technology, or any other company asset. Knowledge is the main resource used in performing work in an organization. The organization's traditions, culture, technology, operations, systems, and procedures are all based on knowledge and expertise. Knowledge is needed to increase the abilities of employees to improve products and services, thereby providing quality service to clients and consumers. Knowledge is necessary to update products and services, change systems and structures, and communicate solutions to problems. In the new knowledge economy, individuals at every level and in all kinds of companies will be challenged to develop new knowledge, to take responsibility for their new ideas, and to pursue them as far as they can go. The job of the leader will be to create an environment that allows workers to increase knowledge.

Knowledge is created continuously in every corner of the globe and doubles every three to four years. One measure of the growth of scientific knowledge is the rate of development of scientific journals. The first two scientific journals appeared in the mid-seventeenth century. By 1750 this number had grown to 10 and by 1800 to approximately 100. Today there are more than 100,000 such journals.

Brainpower is becoming a company's most valuable asset and is what conveys a competitive edge in the marketplace. We are challenged to find and use it. Thomas Stewart asserts, "Brainpower...has never before been so important for business. Every company depends increasingly on knowledge—patents, process, management skills, technologies, information about customers and suppliers, and old-fashioned experience....This knowledge that exists in an organization can be used to create differential advantage. In other words, it's the sum of everything everybody in your company knows that gives you a competitive edge in the marketplace."[22]

Walter Wriston, in *The Twilight of Sovereignty: How the Information Revolution is Transforming the World,* writes that in the end, the location of the new economy is not in technology, be it a microchip or a global communications network, but in the human mind. Robert Reich, U.S. secretary of labor and author of *The Work of Nations,* points out that "corporations no longer focus on products as such; their business strategies increasingly center upon specialized knowledge."[23]

Increasingly, work and learning are becoming the same thing. Because the new global economy is based on knowledge work and innovation, there is a convergence between work and learning. As you perform knowledge work, you learn. And you must learn minute by minute to perform knowledge work effectively. Learning is becoming a lifelong challenge as well as a lifelong process.

In the new economy, the learning component of work becomes huge. It includes everyone from a software developer creating a new multimedia application, to the manager responsible for corporate planning in a bank, to the consultant assessing a client's markets, to the entrepreneur starting up a new business, or to a teaching assistant in a community college.

We are now in the era of knowledge workers. By the beginning of the twenty-first century, three-quarters of the jobs in the U.S. economy involve creating and processing knowledge. Knowledge workers have already discovered that continual learning is not only a prerequisite of employment but is a major form of work. Learning has indeed become the new form of labor.

New Roles and Expectations of Workers. As noted previously, technology and globalization have led to a global economy based on knowledge. Knowledge workers now outnumber industrial workers three to one. The workforce has moved from *manufacturing* (working with the hand) to *mentofacturing* (working with the mind). Continuous learning and knowledge provide the key raw material for wealth creation and have become the fountain of organizational and personal power.

As society moves from the industrial era to the knowledge era, job requirements are changing. Employees are moving from needing repetitive skills to knowing how to deal with surprises and exceptions, from depending on memory and facts to being spontaneous and creative, from risk avoidance to risk taking, from focusing on policies and procedures to building collaborative relationships.

The workforce also has changed. By the year 2000 more than 75 percent of all jobs in the United States were in knowledge/service industries. Many of the new jobs require a much higher level of skill than the jobs they replace, especially in manufacturing and resource-based industries. People retain existing jobs only if they are retrained to higher standards.

The organization of the future will be composed more and more of *knowledge workers*. Not only senior executives but also workers at all levels must be highly educated, highly skilled knowledge workers. In the new postcapitalist society, knowledge is not just another resource alongside the traditional factors of production, land, labor, and capital. It is the only meaningful resource in today's workforce. In an economy based on knowledge, the knowledge worker is the single greatest asset.

A fascinating aspect about knowledge workers is that they do in fact own the means of production, and they can take it out of the door with them at any moment. Therefore, managers have to attract and motivate; reward, recognize, and retain; train, educate, and improve; and, in the most remarkable reversal of all, serve and satisfy knowledge workers. Organizations must provide a structure in which knowledge workers can apply their knowledge. Specifically, organizations must facilitate contact with other knowledge workers because it is through dialogue and interaction with other knowledge workers that they can refine and improve their ideas.

Innovation. Stacey shows that when organizations commit to innovation they enter uncharted waters.[24] As managers have come to recognize the application of chaos theory to organizational development, they realize that no one can know clearly the future of an innovative organization. Accordingly, such organizations discover their destination as they go, and managers in such organizations must develop new strengths and at least partly create their own environments. They must question everything and generate new perspectives through the inquiry process. Such managers see their organizations as a complex web of relationships into which new employees must be incorporated in dynamic ways.

Most managers have been trained to manage for performance rather than for development. Yet managers who manage for performance are more likely to face personnel crises, such as the sudden departure of a star employee for greener pastures or a sense of discouragement that festers when employees believe that the organization is not in their corner. To prevent this managers must focus on developmental issues of their employees and must be available to staff who will come to them to discuss their experience in the organization.[25]

The Merging of Leadership and Management. The idea that leadership is exercised only in the upper ranks of the organization is no longer widely accepted. Companies experience leadership at all levels, and in the networked organization of the future this will become even more common. In rapid-change environments of the twenty-first century, the opportunities for leadership are likely to increase and the distinctions

Table 1.2
Five Degrees of Change

Degree 1	Little change (making goods and services with long product lives)
Degree 2	Continuous improvement (constant incremental changes in products and ways of operating)
Degree 3	Nonincremental change within business (Degree 2 plus regularly introducing new product lines/services and improvements)
Degree 4	Whole new businesses (Degrees 2 and 3 plus inventing whole new businesses as well as new product lines/services)
Degree 5	Whole new business model (Degrees 2, 3, and 4 plus inventing new economic and organizational models)

These changes in organization require accompanying changes in the structure of leadership and management.

Degrees 1–5	Require excellent basic management
Degrees 3–5	Require visionary leadership (plus basic management)
Degrees 4–5	Require energy-unleashing leadership (plus visionary and basic management)

Source: Goldsworthy, A. (2000). *The Heart and Soul of Leadership: Leadership in the Networked World.* Australian Institute of Management.

between management and leadership profiles will blur. In the workplace of the future, the manager's most important focus will be people and knowledge. What managers know will not be as important as how quickly they can learn.

As innovation and change replace stability as dominant characteristics of modern organizations, the roles and responsibilities of managers also change. Kotter offers a model (Five Degrees of Change) to show how the type of leadership necessary for an organization depends on the type and degree of change the organization is undergoing.

Degrees 4 and 5 will come to describe most businesses in the twenty-first century because of the rapid rate of change to the economy, demand, and the changing needs of customers. Companies that are able to operate at levels 4 and 5 will be this century's success stories. Levels 4 and 5 require empowerment of employees as well as visionary leadership and basic management skills. With management ranks generally thinning in organizations, managers increasingly are expected to empower employees and exercise visionary leadership—in short, to be leaders.

Invention of new economic and organizational models will require sustained energy and extraordinary leadership that connect with people's hopes and dreams, their most basic values, and their quest for a meaning in their lives. The leader who would unleash this energy must be adept at role modeling and connecting with the psyche of followers in order to release their great passion and creative power.[26]

Kotter's model suggests that success in the twenty-first century will require a very strong form of transformational leadership reminiscent of Maslow's higher needs of employees: security for self and family, love and respect, opportunities to grow, and a sense of purpose in life. As we shall see, the qualities that the new organization will seek in a manager are the same ones that characterize the mentor. In the sense that leadership is, first and foremost, about empowering others, leadership and mentorship are one and the same.

THE IMPORTANCE OF MENTORING FOR MODERN ORGANIZATIONS

The ascendance of the knowledge age and the transformation of the workplace into an environment of continual learning have made mentoring an increasingly attractive tool for employee development. Companies in which managers mentor as part of the organization's strategy to promote continuous learning promote a number of goals that should mark modern organizations share.

1. **Improvement in job performance:** Mentoring provides for more and better communication with one's manager and more opportunity for the manager to follow an employee's career progress. Such a relationship also results, among all parties, in a deeper attachment to and accountability for one's part in achieving organizational goals.
2. **Acceleration of learning:** With mentoring, employees tend to learn quickly and consequently become productive sooner. Mentors (their managers) can model appropriate behavior, offer specific feedback, and identify best practices.[27]

Howard Rice expects all directors and senior associates to serve as mentors to the more junior attorneys with whom they work. In addition, every associate who starts at the firm, regardless of seniority or experience level, is assigned an associate "buddy" whose express role is to assist the new attorney with the day-to-day concerns of adjusting to work at the firm.[28]

3. **Low turnover:** Many companies have discovered that mentoring new employees helps them settle into their jobs and company environments and contributes to a lower turnover rate.[29] Bell cites the 1999 Emerging Workforce Study, which reported that 35 percent of employees who do not receive a regular mentoring plan look for another job within 12 months.[30]

4. **Empowerment of employees:** Mentoring is strongly associated with self-esteem and with expectations of success. As mentoring is, above all, a social relationship, its power to improve the self-esteem of individuals has long been recognized. Kelly shows that active participation in organized group mentoring is also strongly associated with self-esteem and general expectancy for success.[31]

5. **Promotion of organizational change:** Mentoring focuses on collaboration rather than on command and control. It adds a balance to the overly masculine value culture that has dominated so many companies for years. Abundant evidence exists that values associated with the feminine appeal to organizations in an environment characterized by chaos, openness, flexibility. Avon (see the following case study) is one example of an organization that flourishes in a culture dominated by feminine as well as bottom-line values.

Avon stands out among many companies claiming to be gender-blind meritocracies. Women dominate at nearly every level at this cosmetic and accessory manufacturer and direct seller. Avon features innovative leadership programs and imaginative efforts to retain upper-middle-management women. Its executives are always searching for fresh ways to reinterpret the Avon mission for the latest generation of women managers. In doing so, Avon ensures that it also stays close to its rapidly evolving customer base.[32]

---

6. **Improving the bottom line:** In a knowledge-based economy in which demand shifts constantly and communication is better depicted as a web than as a series of straight lines proceeding from the leader through the ranks, bottom-line concerns require broad participation to insure a company's success. Mentoring can improve the bottom line. According to Mike Pegg, who implemented a mentoring scheme for Microsoft that was ranked second in the 2001 London *Times* best employer list, mentoring results in a positive change in how people communicate long-term company strategy and helps form engaged employees who understand where the company is heading and their roles within it.[33]

BENEFITS OF MENTORING

As mentoring schemes are typically instituted to promote learning, productivity, and retention of employees, the benefits to the mentors and to the organization may be overlooked. Those involved with mentoring generally agree that benefits accrue to mentees, mentors, and organizations.

Mentees

Mentees are the most obvious beneficiaries. Workplace mentoring has become valuable for them for a number of reasons:

- It speeds up learning. Mentees become more mature and productive sooner because they learn more quickly from mentors who can provide shortcuts, best practices, reality checks, live modeling, and detailed feedback that books or classrooms can not.
- It transfers integrated knowledge. Engstrøm shows that mentoring is a powerful tool to facilitate the sharing of tacit knowledge, that personal integration of knowledge and experience leads to formation of belief, values, and wisdom.[34] In the dynamic of trust and sharing that characterizes the mentor/mentee relationship, tacit knowledge passes freely.
- It is a perk. Even with limited budgets, organizations still want to attract performers. Furthermore, as we have seen, many organizations point to cost savings achieved through mentoring.
- It enhances careers. Many new college graduates seek assurances that their employment experience will add to their development, and recruiters report that organizations with mentoring in place have an edge over competitors.

My greatest challenge was in securing the National Science Foundation grant that launched Kit & Kaboodle. I had never written a grant proposal before so I had to learn how while finding a way to communicate the value of my idea. I learned the importance of Sir Isaac Newton's philosophy that he accomplished what he did by standing on the shoulders of giants. Mentors who believed in my ideas and my abilities helped me learn what I needed to know, guided my efforts, and encouraged my persistence.

—Sandra Markle, president, CompuQuest, Inc.

Mentors

Mentors, according to most studies, report more satisfaction from the mentoring relationship than mentees. Mentors benefit from the opportunity to practice and enhance their management and development skills and to have contact with people who may be different culturally or in age from themselves. Specifically, mentors receive:

- recognition from peers and superiors for hard work, a successful career, and demonstrated leadership skills;
- opportunities to expand horizons;
- opportunities to network with others;
- opportunities to learn from protégés;
- practice with interpersonal and leadership skills;
- opportunities to review and validate what they have learned; and
- opportunities to recharge their batteries.

Those who are not natural mentors have the opportunity to improve their communication skills and their ability to develop colleagues. Another advantage for a mentor may result when the mentee, who remembers the power of the mentoring experience and the kindness and skill of the mentor, ascends to the top of the organization.

Mentoring can revitalize a manager's interest in work and fulfill his or her own developmental needs. Interacting with a new person with different work experiences will stimulate thinking and provide a fresh perspective. In addition, mentors develop coaching, feedback, planning, and career development skills.

The mentor can also receive assistance in completing work. Mentors can suggest activities that help them in their work and are developmental to employees. Mentors commonly report as a benefit to themselves the opportunity to share their experience and make a contribution to the development of another person. They enjoy seeing their mentees grow and learn.

Organizations

Organizations realize benefits from mentoring as well. According to Wedin, mentoring has specifically benefited organizations in the following areas:[35]

- cultural change,
- establishment of a diverse workforce,
- succession planning,
- recruitment and retention of employees,

- orientation of new employees,
- development of employees with high potential, and
- transition to international assignments.

Procter & Gamble (P&G) offers an example of how an organization has used mentoring to accomplish cultural change by providing experiences through mentoring to women who traditionally had to advance through staff positions instead of line positions, leaving them less qualified for eventual movement into senior management positions.[36]

Mentoring can help retain valuable employees in an environment in which organizations are losing collective wisdom. As the baby boom generation moves toward retirement, many organizations anticipate the loss of highly experienced employees. For example, the U.S. Veterans Health Administration (VHA) reported in 2003 that 65 percent of its executive nurses would be eligible to retire in five years.[37] With these retirees will go decades of wisdom, stories, history and traditions, deeply held core values, and a host of skills. The VHA and other government agencies such as National Aeronautic and Space Agency (NASA) are developing leadership mentoring initiatives that link potential retirees with a variety of mentee audiences.[38]

Organizations that manage their own mentoring programs report that these programs are a cost-effective way to develop staff and build skills and experience throughout the company. In particular, they are able to retain graduates by managing their expectations, channeling their ambitions, and maintaining their levels of motivation. Even companies that rely on external agents to run their mentoring programs draw high-quality applicants to the company. This is particularly important for organizations wanting to attract potential managers from minority ethnic groups underrepresented in the organization.

Janas cites additional benefits of mentoring to organizations.[39] Mentoring:

- increases access to the pool of expertise within an organization.
- increases productivity. Mentoring improves and increases skills for both the mentor and the employee. Multiskilled people increase efficiency and productivity in an organization.
- improves communication. By its nature, mentoring facilitates communication across management levels. If the mentor and employee come from different functional divisions or groups, communication can be improved across these organizational boundaries as well.

- is an effective succession planning strategy. It can contribute to recruitment, retention, knowledge transfer, and workforce development. Mentoring also can contribute to the promotion of diversity in an organization.
- maximizes an organization's training budget by providing more knowledge to employees with little direct cost.
- sets a positive example for future supervisors, managers, and tomorrow's leaders.

According to *Business Week* (March 1, 1999), Interim Services and Louis Harris and Associates conducted a survey that measured the cost of not mentoring employees and providing poor training. The article stated: "Among employees who say their company offers poor training, 41% plan to leave within a year, vs. only 12% of those who rate opportunities excellent. High turnover isn't cheap. The survey pegs the cost of losing a typical worker at $50,000."[40]

Some small businesses may be reluctant to adopt mentoring programs, fearing they will take time away from business and lower productivity. But companies must set these concerns against the evidence that mentoring enhances relationships in teams, stimulates motivation, and develops business skills. Both the Small Business Administration and the U.S. Army have mentoring programs for owners of small businesses who can not invest in schemes of their own.

Other trends such as downsizing, restructuring, teamwork, increased diversity, and individual responsibility for career development have threatened organizations' needs to preserve institutional memory and to keep experiential knowledge within the company and have contributed to the resurgence of mentoring. Mentors represent continuity; older, experienced workers, as mentors, can continue contributing to their organizations and professions. The Mentoring Institute has described a new mentoring paradigm wherein mentees, although better educated, still need a mentor's practical know-how and wisdom that can be acquired only experientially. Many organizations believe that formal mentoring programs are a cost-effective way to upgrade skills, enhance recruitment and retention, and increase job satisfaction.[41]

CHALLENGES TO MANAGERS AS MENTORS IN THE TWENTY-FIRST CENTURY

As companies increasingly turn to managers as mentors for the development of staff, managers find themselves facing a number of obstacles.

An Increasingly Diverse Work Experience

In a global economy, diverse workplaces are becoming more common. Yet, managing across differences is one of the most difficult and important challenges any manager can face. Without conscious and sustained effort, relationships in a diverse workplace are unlikely to be developmental. If differences are suppressed rather than celebrated and discussed openly, the manager's feedback to the employee is less likely to be of value toward the employee's development.

If managers do not have a global or international background, they may find it difficult to manage the career objectives and the performance of foreign citizens working in the United States. Dean Foster, managing director of Berlitz Cross-Cultural Division Worldwide, an international cultural training firm, says many non-Americans working within the United States struggle with what are uniquely American ways of doing things. For example, in the U.S. workplace, individuals are encouraged to be self-starters and achieve goals independently. But many other cultures do not work that way.

"One of the biggest complaints we hear from non-Americans working in the United States is that they feel abandoned—they feel they get no direction and are not trained properly," says Foster. "They feel like they are completely lost in a very impersonal structure in an environment that assumes they will do things on their own and achieve on their own."[42]

Managers of global companies sometimes fail to understand that employees from abroad need a great deal of direction and support. This next generation of global business leaders needs help to work through problems and reach the right conclusions. One of the best ways to assist them is to assign mentors to guide them.[43]

A Culture of Greed and Individualism

Reports of flagrant misbehavior among leaders at the corporate, government, and even nonprofit levels over the past 20 years point to a mind set that considers success as that which allows the individual to use organizational power for the achievement of personal goals. Too often these personal agendas have included amassing wealth and personal power far beyond that required for a secure and purposeful life. At worst, they have dashed the expectations of millions of employees for rewarding work and modest pensions to support them in their older years.

An environment of individual aggrandizement eventually dooms a company's chances to contribute to the betterment of society and undermines the very premises of the value of mentoring—its commitment to trust, listening to and valuing the opinions of others, collaboration in achieving organizational goals, and putting oneself at the service of those who will lead the organization into the future.

Many organizations are led by people imbued with public purpose and with the sense of themselves in service to others. They signify that arrogance and greed do not have to be identified as hallmarks of business. Their behavior is associated with servant leadership, and a growing number of businesses are drawing from this model. Among the top 100 best companies to work for, according to *Fortune* magazine, more than 20 percent have sought guidance from the Greenleaf Center, a not-for-profit institution chartered to help people understand the principles and practices of servant leadership.[44]

Overwork

In May 2001 the Families and Work Institute, supported by PricewaterhouseCoopers, released a study entitled, *Feeling Overworked: When Work Becomes Too Much.* Nearly half (46%) of the respondents reported feeling overworked, overwhelmed by the amount of work they faced, or that there was not enough time to reflect on their work. Respondents gave many reasons for these feelings.

- Working long hours to meet employer expectations.
- Working more than one prefers.
- Experiencing on-the-job pressures.
- Multitasking too much.
- Using technology for work during nonwork time.
- Being accessible to an employer during nonwork time.
- Using less of their vacation time because of work demands.
- Working for an organization that has downsized or has had difficulty hiring.
- Having a job with less job autonomy, more wasted time, fewer learning opportunities, and less job security.
- Working in less supportive workplaces.

The study confirmed that demands on overworked employees affect job performance, relationships, and health. The more overworked employees feel, the more likely they are to make mistakes at work, feel angry toward their employers, and look for a new job with another employer. Moreover, employees who feel overworked tend to experience more work/life conflict; feel less successful in relationships with spouse/partner, children, and friends; sleep less; feel less healthy and more stressed; neglect themselves; and feel less able to cope with everyday life events.

Those reporting the longest work weeks are not distinguished by their occupations, but by the kinds of jobs they hold. Specifically, managers and professionals report longer work hours far in excess of any other job category, among both men and women.

But working is not its own reward, even for managers and professionals. In a 1997 survey conducted by the Families and Work Institute, 60 percent of both men and women workers responded that they would like to work less.[45] According to Net Futures Institute, a U.S.-based research firm that identifies and analyzes trends and attitudes in business, organizational management, and information technology, longer hours spent on the job by mangers does not necessarily have a positive impact on employees. As managers work longer and feel overworked, 2,000 senior executives and managers across the United States report that employee morale is going down.[46]

Traditional Preparation of Managers

The global workforce teems with millions of managers who were neither prepared nor selected as managers for their role as mentors. Yet mentors are expected to serve as a role models, sponsors, encouragers, counselors, and friends to less skilled or less experienced personnel for the purposes of promoting the latter's professional and/or personal development.[47]

WHY MANAGERS NEED TO BECOME MENTORS

How then will a manager who was not trained to mentor, and who may already feel overworked, welcome the opportunity to mentor others in the organization? First, managers must understand that mentoring is part of a broader organizational commitment to empower employees, to develop their capacity for learning and leadership, and to increase their confidence and commitment to contribute to the organization. Mentoring programs should improve the initiative and productivity of employees and lighten the manager's workload.

Second, successful mentoring behavior can be taught.[48] Training in communication and active listening techniques, relationship skills, effective teaching, models of supervision and coaching, conflict resolution, and problem solving are areas that are often included in workshops for mentors.[49]

Not everyone will make a good mentor. Although companies may assume that managers should automatically be able to perform the mentor's role, in practice many managers are unable to escape from their command-and-control habits. Others lack the depth of self-awareness that characterizes an effective mentor.

Great care should be taken in the selection and preparation of managers who will mentor. Insofar as possible, mentees should have some choice in who will be their mentors. Ideally, a program coordinator offers a selection of possible mentors, from which the mentee chooses. In this way, the mentee feels some ownership of the relationship and how it is to be managed. Selection by mentors often does not work well and should be avoided.[50]

"Well, Wendy, the training was pretty good. We focused on listening and feedback skills and got involved in role-play, dealing with mentoring situations. I really didn't realize until now that mentoring is about learning rather than performance."

"I wish my mentee, Karl, understood that," said Wendy. "I think he is intimidated by women and has to show how well he can perform. I get the feeling he is just using mentoring to fast-track his career. But I don't think he is committed to learning."

"Didn't you tell me that you have a mentoring agreement?" Wayne asked.

"Yes, and I am going to have to confront him with it when we next meet. I think we need to review what we want from this partnership and how we are going to get there."

"Good luck," said Wayne. "My mentoring coordinator has been doing matchups and I will learn my mentee's identity tomorrow. I hope he's a Red Sox fan!"

"In your dreams, Wayne."

They both had a good laugh.

MENTORING AND THE IDEAL WORKPLACE OF THE TWENTY-FIRST CENTURY

According to a recent Development Dimensions International (DDI) survey, in the ideal workplace of the twenty-first century, employees control resources, systems, methods, working conditions, and work schedules. Leaders build an environment of trust by listening to and communicating with employees. Shared vision and values help guide decision making. Decision making occurs at the lowest level. Individuals have the ability and data to measure their own performance and progress. Leaders and associates work together to establish clear goals, expectations, and accountabilities. Leaders champion continuous improvement, facilitate learning, and reinforce effective performance. Risk taking is encouraged and mistakes are treated as learning opportunities. Performance feedback comes from peers, customers, and direct reports. Systems—selection and promotion, rewards and recognition, compensation, information management, and so forth—are aligned to reinforce and drive desired behaviors. Effective training is provided to build skills at the teachable moment (just-in-time), and jobs are designed to provide employee ownership and responsibility.

As we will see in the chapters that follow, mentoring has the power to create and sustain such a workplace. Organizations in which managers serve as mentors become organizations of learning, productivity, and high employee satisfaction. New opportunities to significantly impact the world of work await the mentoring manager.

TWO

New Trends and Issues in Mentoring

As we begin the twenty-first century we are witnessing an exponential increase in the velocity, complexity, and unpredictability of change. Change marks our major institutions, our communities, and our workspace; impacts global relationships; and creates a hypercompetitive international environment that bears little resemblance to the one that existed even five years ago.

In this environment mentoring has been revived because formal educational systems have not yet caught up with the rapid pace of global change. Mentoring helps develop and reinforce self-directed learning, builds confidence, stimulates loyalty to the organization, clarifies career goals, builds leadership competencies, and promotes teamwork.

Changes wrought by the speed of information dissemination and the increasing rate of knowledge production have had a profound impact on mentoring, on how it is done, and on the issues it addresses. This chapter will examine how mentoring has adapted to the learning needs of adults; new trends in the workplace; the various mentoring models and how they addresses learning, leadership development, career development, and retention; and the matching of mentor and mentee.

MENTORING AND ADULT LEARNING

The theory of adult learning developed by Malcolm Knowles more than 40 years ago remains one of the most comprehensive and best known. Knowles's theory is based on four assumptions:

- Adults need to be self-directed learners. Adults learn best when they are involved in diagnosing, planning, implementing, and evaluating their own learning. Adults respond best to learning when they are internally motivated to learn.
- The experiential base of adults is a rich resource for learning, and the life experiences of others enrich the learning process.
- Learning is linked to what adults need to know or do in order to fulfill their roles and responsibilities. Adult learners have an inherent need for immediacy of application, and readiness for learning increases when there is a specific need to know.
- Adult learners are problem centered rather than subject centered.

Mentors must be sensitive to these needs and create a supportive climate that promotes conditions necessary for learning to take place.

"Wayne, I need some advice about Karl."

"Look, Wendy. You are a much stronger mentor than I am. I don't know what I can offer you."

"Well, since I confronted Karl four weeks ago, things have been going very well. He has been focused and more open to learning opportunities. And that is part of my problem."

"What do you mean?" asked Wayne.

"I recommended two weeks ago that he call Bob in Operations Planning because Karl said he wants to learn more about that part of the organization. But he hasn't done it. Maybe he is timid about calling a senior manager. Do you think I should make the appointment for him? I hate to see him spin his wheels."

"I don't think so, Wendy. Maybe he changed his mind. How about just asking him? And if he is timid, ask him how he thinks he might overcome his timidity."

"Gee, Wayne, that's good idea! And you were worried that you weren't cut out for this!"

"Well, I have been comparing notes with other managers who are mentoring, and I am learning a lot from them. But I have an issue, too."

"What is it?"

"Jocelyn really has had some good ideas about dealing with the general public, ideas good enough to bring to senior staff. I'm thinking about inviting her to senior staff meeting to talk about this. You know, even though there is no rule against bringing a staff member to senior staff meetings, it is almost never done."

Wendy smiled. "That's because the senior staff want to claim great ideas as their own."

"That's a bit cynical, Wendy, though I am aware there are staff who don't share good ideas because they don't believe they will get credit for them."

"Well it would be a great learning experience for your mentee and you would come across as the wonderful, empowering, and humble guy that you are."

"Yeah, right," said Wayne, smiling. "But I might just do it."

Self-Directed Learning

Among Knowles's assumptions about adult learning, his notion of self-directed learning has particular importance to mentoring. Self-directed learning means that the adult learner controls his education at any given point in time. This enhances the learner's intrinsic being as well as the life and well-being of others and society at large. Self-directed learning provides a liberating perspective for the learner because it brings both the intellectual and social learning environment into the learner's critical awareness and social interactions.[1]

This approach to learning is the bedrock of the mentoring process. Learning is most effective when situated in a context in which new knowledge and skills will be used, and learners construct meaning for themselves within the context of interaction with others. Mentors facilitate learning by encouraging learners in the spirit of inquiry and by modeling problem-solving strategies. Mentors gradually decrease their assistance as learners internalize these behaviors and construct their own knowledge and understanding. These processes are reflected in the mentor's roles of guide, adviser, coach, motivator, facilitator, and role model within a contextual setting. Mentors provide authentic, experiential learning opportunities as well as an intense interpersonal relationships through which social learning takes place.[2]

MENTORING MODELS

One of the goals of many formal mentoring programs is to bring the organization to the point at which the majority of mentoring is carried out informally, without the need for substantial, structured support from HR and elsewhere. The problem, in most cases, is that completely informal mentoring—in which people come together without guidance and without clarity about the mentoring role—is a hit-and-miss affair. Not only is the quality of the relationships highly variable, but the pairings tend to exclude people who do not fit the mold, by virtue of their gender, race, culture, or some other differentiating factor.[3]

Formal mentoring programs are increasingly popular, partly because of reported benefits of the arrangement. Mentees often describe the relationship as a positive one in which they can talk in confidence with a professional outside of their project teams on matters of professional growth and development. Mentors report positive feelings about the opportunity to give something back to the profession in terms of assisting a junior colleague to move along the career path.[4]

The changes in the conditions of work described in chapter 1 have been matched by the development of various mentoring models. Table 2.1 shows the correspondence of these trends and the accompanying mentoring models that are used.

As globalization has compressed time and space, so has the traditional multiple-year mentoring relationship yielded to shorter connections and to multiple mentors, successive or simultaneous. Various mentoring models have developed in response to changing workplace needs. These include: (1) virtual, or long distance, mentoring; (2) cross-cultural men-

Table 2.1
Workplace Trends and Mentoring Models

Workplace Trend	Mentoring Model in Use
Learning organization	Communities of practice
Advances in technology	Virtual mentoring
Globalization and diversity	Virtual mentoring; cross-cultural mentoring
Ascendance of knowledge	Communities of practice; peer mentoring; mentoring among organizations; action learning
New roles and expectations of workers	Virtual mentoring; successive mentoring; communities of practice
Merging of leadership and management	Action learning; communities of practice
Changes in the workplace	Virtual mentoring; mentoring among organizations
Innovation	Action learning; virtual mentoring; peer mentoring

toring; (3) group mentoring, in which mentors facilitate the learning of a group of mentees; (4) peer mentoring, in which groups and pairs mentor one another; and (5) organizational mentoring, in which intact business mentoring teams help fledgling businesses. Each of these is examined in the following sections.

VIRTUAL MENTORING

Face-to-face mentoring is the most common form of mentoring, but circumstances in modern organizations have made virtual mentoring more popular. Sometimes called long-distance mentoring or "telementoring," virtual mentoring uses videoconferencing, the Internet, and e-mail to mentor individuals or companies. This can appeal to those who own small businesses and are unable to leave their workplace or those who live in rural or remote communities. Virtual mentoring is usually less expensive than face-to-face mentoring and provides an individual with more choices for mentors. Virtual mentoring is greatly enhanced by at least one meeting between mentor and mentee and may suffer considerably if a meeting does not take place.

One of the challenges for any mentoring program is time. Face-to-face mentoring requires that both people involved be available at the same time. With virtual mentoring, however, time is a less limiting factor, as it is not necessary for both participants to be available at the same time. Hansen notes that in his Saskatchewan Valley Mentoring Project he and his mentees had families and full-time jobs and no extra time to spare.[5] Correspondence allowed both mentors and mentees to communicate at a time that was convenient, which might be late in the evening or on weekends after chores.

A virtual mentoring program provides for greater flexibility in place as well as in time. Hansen's mentoring project, based at the University of Saskatchewan in Saskatoon, involved participants who lived more than 150 miles apart. Hansen notes that although media richness theory suggests that virtual mentoring does not provide adequate feedback capability, his experience was that a mentee's willingness to give feedback increases when the feedback does not need to be delivered face-to-face. His mentees gave him both positive and negative feedback throughout the duration of the program.

Limitations of a Virtual Mentoring Program

Virtual mentoring can mitigate time and distance constraints, yet it is difficult to produce the intimacy and spontaneity of interpersonal communication that usually develops in face-to-face mentoring. If the partners permit weeks to go by without contact, either or both may lose enthusiasm for the relationship. Virtual mentoring may not afford the richness in communication between participants as does face-to-face mentoring. Those involved in virtual mentoring, although recognizing its value, usually urge the provision of some face-to-face time.[6]

CROSS-CULTURAL MENTORING

Cross-cultural mentoring broadly refers to mentoring partnerships that involve differences in gender, age, or race/ethnicity or nationality. Culture is a strong determinant of behavior, values, and communication. All of the following, for example, are determined by culture:

- deference to authority,
- expressions of power,
- individualism/collectivism,
- conflict management,
- assertiveness,
- frankness,
- self-promotion, and
- importance of personal relationships.[7]

General Mills Co-Mentoring

We believe that diverse teams create more and better solutions. A diverse workforce helps us stay ahead of our competitors through growth and innovation.

At General Mills, the Corporate Mentoring Program is designed to support development, motivation, and retention and to prepare employees to move into managerial roles. This program pairs employees of color and new managers with an experienced General Mills employee. The program helps to formally connect new minority employees with senior-level mentors in the company. Exposed to different parts of the company, these employees establish greater connections throughout the organization.

The program also promotes a cross-functional, two-way learning exchange and dialogue between the two partners, who serve as both mentor and mentee within the relationship, and generates a broader awareness of gender and racial issues at the most senior levels of the company.

Forty-five partnerships were established in 2000, consisting of General Mills officers who were paired with director-level and higher women or people of color. These 45 pairs reached deep into the 79 officers at General Mills and included both vice chairmen.

General Mills has won numerous awards for employer of choice, including "Top 50 Companies for Latinas to Work in the U.S." and "100 Best Companies for Working Mothers."[8] In 2001, GM was recognized with the Catalyst Award for outstanding initiatives for the advancement of women in the workplace.

Studies of African American executives show a direct correlation between having mentors and job growth, promotions, and salary increases.

- Not having an influential mentor or sponsor was reported as one of the top barriers to advancement of African American female executives, according to *Catalyst*'s 2002 "Women of Color in Corporate Management Report."
- The same study also shows that 69 percent of those with mentors were promoted, compared with 50 percent of those with no mentors.
- According to Korn/Ferry International's 1998 study *Diversity in the Executive Suite: Creating Successful Career Paths and Strategies,* formal and informal mentoring and support from superiors and coworkers are key factors that help place minority executives on the organizational fast track.
- Korn/Ferry International's study also shows that African American executives who reported having informal mentors at work (73 percent) had faster salary and total compensation growth than those without one.[9]

Although mentoring among minority groups continues to be used as a remedy to address discrimination in the workplace, cross-cultural mentoring both includes and transcends issues of race.

PricewaterhouseCoopers (UK)

PwC goal: Creating an environment that enables all our people to realize their full potential

In 2002, PricewaterhouseCoopers (PwC) identified barriers to women's advancement in the organization and the practical steps that must be taken to address them. PwC created a women's network with the following objectives:

- Empower people to maximize their potential.
- Support the recruitment and retention of the most talented people.
- Raise the visibility of role models through:
  - development of local satellite and e-networks,
  - mentoring programs, and
  - networks.
- Assist in succession planning.
- Help address issues relating to changing demographics.
- Enable the organization to mirror the diverse cultures of clients.
- Dispel myths, communicate, and inform.

PwC established Mentoring Connections as a key initiative to meet these objectives. Though Mentoring Connections, as part of a wider mentoring program developed by the network, is available to men and women, all board members mentor at least one senior woman. This initiative puts women in touch with female role models across the organization.

Since establishing the Women's Network, PwC has:

- increased the quantity of contracts it has won,
- appointed its first woman board member,
- doubled the number of women on the supervisory board,
- increased the percentage of women in senior positions and director roles, and
- increased by 10 percent (to 72.6 percent) the belief among women that the organization is committed to becoming a great place to work.

Through Mentoring Connections, men in the organization have gained a better understanding of the impact their behavior can have on women, and all employees have closer contact with key decision makers within the organization.

PwC was the winner of the Opportunity Now Innovation Award for 2004, given by Business in the Community (BITC), a coalition of more than 2,000 businesses around the world that encourages the business community to have a positive impact on society.

Cross-cultural barriers are embedded in and expressed by language, but a more basic chasm has to do with how one sees the world and how one acts within it. In China, for example, the role of teacher is traditionally revered in the Confucian order of hierarchy and status ranking, and one's perception of the teacher can limit openness and directness of communication and influence how conflict is resolved. Accountability is also linked to cultural perceptions. In some cultures, the expectation is that the teacher must initiate contact, and communication is tied to credibility and control.

The success of a cross-cultural mentoring relationship requires a number of conditions:

- a mentor's cross-cultural competency,
- a flexible cultural lens,
- well-honed communication skills, and
- an authentic desire to understand how culture affects the individuals engaged in this relationship.

Many of the competencies needed to establish successful global relationships in business pertain to mentoring relationships as well. These include becoming culturally self-aware, developing a working knowledge of and appreciation for other cultures, improving communications skills, and becoming culturally attuned to other cultures.[10]

"So, how did it go with your mentee?"

"Oh, I am very pleased," said Wendy. "At the beginning of our last meeting I told Karl I was concerned that I was not meeting his needs. I asked that we review our mentoring partnership agreement to reorient ourselves. Then I asked how he felt it was going and how he thought I could be more helpful. To my surprise, he admitted that he hadn't been fully committed to the partnership and was trying to act like he didn't need a mentor. I guess he meant he didn't need my help. I told him that mentoring matches don't always work and that if he felt he might do better with another mentor, I would help him find one."

"Wow," said Wayne.

"But then he said he had a mentor before and it didn't work well. He realized that he needed to look at his own motivation and asked me to help him work this through."

"Nice job, Wendy!"

"No, I just gave him permission to make his own decision about this. Karl is like so many younger workers I have run across. He is very smart, very bright but hasn't developed a vision for his life. So, Wayne, how is it going with your mentee?"

"I thought we would have been matched by gender and race, but neither of those things happened. But Jocelyn does like baseball, and her sense of humor is sort of like mine."

"Uh-oh," said Wendy.

"Actually, we have become comfortable enough after just two meetings that I dared to ask her today if she had expected someone different from me."

"What did she say to that?" asked Wendy.

"She said that my work in public relations was exactly what she envisioned for herself and that she had asked others about my style as a manager and about my ability to communicate."

"Oh my, she has done her homework," said Wendy.

"Well, she said she felt she could learn a lot from me and was pleased with the match. At her suggestion we are going to spend the next session going over her learning goals for the mentorship."

"Wow, this sounds good, Wayne! But not so much like the federal workers who don't put out much effort," Wendy smiled.

"Yeah, I was probably too harsh. I just hope I can keep up with her."

GROUP AND PEER MENTORING

Group mentoring may have particular appeal to companies in which the number of potential mentees far exceeds the availability of mentors or in which there is an interest in beginning the mentoring process on as large a scale as possible. Under the guidance of an experienced mentor, mentees may be encouraged to assist one another with their learning goals. The active involvement of mentees with one another's learning in a group setting is often referred to as peer mentoring.

For many workers, the most effective learning experiences are the informal sharing of knowledge between peers who perform similar functions or who participate in a series of integrated processes. Peer mentoring is usually informal, but organizations can recognize and support the mutual learning that is involved in peer mentoring.

Two group mentoring approaches that have proven particularly effective in achieving learning objectives of members include action learning and communities of practice.

Action Learning

As a formal learning process and as a method of leadership development, action learning is an excellent vehicle for group mentoring. As group members focus on their learning needs, both the action learning coach and the group members function as mentors. The powerful method of inquiry at the heart of action learning both broadens and deepens the learning of the group members, even as it reinforces leadership development and systems thinking.

Action learning is steeped in the understanding that questions are always more powerful than statements in solving problems and in deepening the learning process. Questions require that we listen carefully and reflect. They demonstrate our ability to empathize and care about others. Questions can motivate as much or more than exhortatory statements. They cause us and the people around us to think, to learn, and to grow.[11]

Among the many types of questions that mentors and mentees can pose, the best are those that generate the most reflection and learning. And the very best may require that the group members mull it over during the time between they meet. All members can ask reflective questions, but mentors have a special responsibility to deepen mentees' learning. Examples of reflective questions are given in chapter 6.

Communities of Practice

Communities of practice can exist in any organization. These communities, often unofficial, are not bound by organizational affiliations; rather they span institutional structures and hierarchies. They can be found:

- **within businesses.** Communities of practice arise as people address recurring sets of problems together. Recruiters, account executives, or claims processors within an office or organization may form communities of practice to deal with the constant flow of information they need to process and the decisions they need to make.
- **across business units.** People who work cross-functionally form communities of practice to keep in touch with their peers in various parts of the company and maintain their expertise. When communities of practice cut across business units, they can develop strategic perspectives that transcend the fragmentation of product lines. For instance, a community of practice may propose a plan for equipment purchase that no one business unit could have come up with on its own.
- **across company boundaries.** In some cases, communities of practice cross organizational boundaries. For instance, in fast-moving industries engineers who work for suppliers and buyers may form a community of practice to keep up with constant technological changes.

Communities of practice create, accumulate, and diffuse knowledge in organizations. They become essential to:

- **exchange and interpretation of information.** Because members have a shared understanding, they know what is relevant to communicate and how to present information in useful ways. They move information and share best practices, tips, or feedback across organizational boundaries.

- **knowledge retention.** Unlike a database or a manual, communities of practice adapt knowledge to local circumstances and preserve the tacit aspects of knowledge that formal systems cannot capture.
- **stewardship of competencies.** Members of these groups discuss novel ideas, work together on problems, and keep up with developments inside and outside a firm. Their collaborative inquiry molds their professional identities as part of a dynamic, forward-looking community.
- **ongoing identity.** Communities of practice are not as temporary as teams, and unlike business units, they are organized around what matters to their members. Their identity helps them to focus on what is important and becomes central to learning in the organization. Communities of practice structure an organization's learning potential in two ways: through the knowledge they develop at their core and through interactions at their boundaries.

As an expression of peer mentoring, communities of practice do not usually require heavy institutional infrastructures, but their members do need time and space to collaborate. They do not require much management, but they can use leadership. They self-organize, but they flourish when their learning fits with their organizational environment. Managers may assist peer mentoring groups by proposing problems to be solved and by assisting these groups to reflect on their learning, thus deepening it and making it applicable to other organizational problems and issues.

The task for managers is to help such communities find resources and connections without overwhelming them with organizational meddling. This need for balance reflects the following paradox: No community can fully design the learning of another; conversely, no community can fully design its own learning.[12]

MENTORING AMONG ORGANIZATIONS

The use of mentoring for business training is not new, even though the structures of mentoring have changed to meet the changes in corporate organizational structures and practice. Broader cultural changes occasioned by the knowledge age have had an impact on the extent and uses of mentoring. One of these is business-to-business mentoring. Companies may also enter into mentoring relationships for a variety of reasons: (1) to receive personalized information and assistance, (2) to gain free or low cost information, (3) to acquire industry-specific information, and (4) to learn new ideas that may save money or address a specific issue.

Environmental mentoring is a relatively new approach to transferring environmental management knowledge. Environmental mentoring focuses on cultivating improved environmental performance through the interaction between business peers. Examples include:

- General Motors Lean Implementation Program mentors suppliers on environmental and other key business issues. GM's Supplier Environmental Advisory Team offers feedback from key suppliers to help shape GM's environmental initiatives.
- The John Roberts Company mentors small printing companies on compliance and pollution prevention issues under the guidance of the U.S. Environmental Protection Agency's Environmental Leadership Program.
- Pittsburgh Business Efficiency Partnership mentors a broad sector of Pittsburgh, Pennsylvania, industries via workshops on energy efficiency and other environmental issues.
- Santa Clara County Pollution Prevention Program mentors printed circuit board and metal finishing companies by offering workshops on emerging pollution prevention technologies.
- WasteCap of Massachusetts mentors, via site visits and other technical assistance, Massachusetts businesses interested in solid waste reduction.

The Institute for Corporate Environmental Monitoring (ICEM) has documented benefits to a number of companies that participated in corporate environmental mentoring programs:

- Best Feeds cut electrical usage by 70 percent in the warehouse area for a cost savings of $2,000 a month and reduced solid waste by half, saving at least $400,000 per year.
- Bromley Printing cut its hazardous and solid waste generation by switching chemicals and increasing recycling of various wastes. These measures resulted in an 87 percent reduction in hauling charges, from $180 per month to $24 per month.
- BASF Automotive made operational changes that significantly reduced energy consumption for a cost savings of $20,000 per year.

According to ICEM, mentor companies also benefit from participating in mentoring programs. These benefits can include meeting specific business objectives, such as improving environmental performance of a supplier, demonstrating leadership in an industry or community, and raising performance of an entire industry sector.

Companies that sponsor and/or participate in mentoring activities also appear to benefit from sharing information and demonstrating leadership within an industry sector and community as they help raise the performance standards of the industry sector.[13]

Sir Speedy

Learning from larger businesses

When Mark Jacobs, the co-owner of Bloomfield, Connecticut's Sir Speedy wanted to expand his business, he wasn't sure where to turn for expert advice. He worried about negotiating a deal that could cost close to $1 million.

Fortunately, Jacobs reached out to John Giamalis, senior vice president and treasurer at The Hartford. Giamalis introduced Jacobs to Joe Boures, a senior-level merger and acquisitions expert at The Hartford. Over several months Boures worked with Jacobs to structure a deal to buy Sir Speedy centers in Vernon and Windsor Locks. Through this mentoring relationship, Jacobs gained access to other financial, legal, and accounting resources at The Hartford. Boures also helped Jacobs think through ways to consolidate expenses and service an expanded customer base.

Today, with the deal complete, Mark Jacobs's business is 50 percent larger, with more cash flow, greater market penetration, a more diverse customer base, and greater financial stability.

Jacobs's story is one of the successes of the relatively new Connecticut chapter of the national BusinessLINC program. BusinessLINC matches experienced business mentors from large companies with minority-owned businesses to help nurture and guide burgeoning companies. In 2003, the program's first year in the state, seven BusinessLINC one-on-one mentoring relationships were established; in 2004, 22 were set up.

BusinessLINC involves a one-year commitment, including at least monthly contact. The $50 application requires the small business to explain what challenge or issue it wants to try to resolve via the BusinessLINC program. Each mentoring relationship receives a midyear and a final evaluation by an executive from another mentoring company.

Alice Byrd, president of Turner Training, who is mentored by Ivan Gutierrez, director of corporate services for Northwest Utilities, calls her mentoring relationship ideal and "a match made in heaven." She says, "It's a wonderful opportunity for me to learn and grow."

BusinessLINC helps both the mentored small business and the mentoring company. "The large corporations who provide the mentoring gain real-time, accurate information about what's going on in the small-business world and what's going on in the urban communities. That's very valuable information," says Fred McKinney, president of the Connecticut Minority Supplier Development Council.

Jacobs advises potential mentees to make sure they know what they want from the program before they apply. "My partner and I had great success with BusinessLINC because we knew what we wanted out of the program," he says. "If you just say, 'Gee, it would nice to have a mentor' and you have no goals or objectives, it's probably not going to work as well for you as it did for us."

MENTORING AND LEADERSHIP DEVELOPMENT

One of the most frequently asked questions about mentoring in business is "Can managers be mentors?" In chapter 1, we noted the merging of leadership and management as organizations thinned the ranks of middle management. As middle managers acquire and enhance leadership skills, they also develop their capacity for mentoring. Being an effective manager today requires an ability to build people, not just production and systems.

In the early days of the industrial age, bosses generally did not ask employees their opinions but simply told them what to do. As work became more complex, workers' value increased and the managerial class evolved to guide the workforce toward the accomplishment of organizational goals. Measurement techniques were developed to determine skill and production levels of workers, who were rewarded based on their individual productivity.

With the advent of the age of knowledge and the growing need for skilled knowledge workers, the manager's role changed to include meeting the learning needs of workers and managing the impact of new knowledge. The new generation of workers expects more of their bosses than just assignments and rewards. They want to feel that they are part of accomplishing something worthwhile and that they are valued by the people they work for. Businesses have reduced the number of available management positions and have more people ready for promotions than promotional opportunities.

This situation poses new challenges for managers who need to be able to find, keep, and develop talented people who work out of commitment rather than compliance. To be successful today, managers have to become mentors too.

This means that managers must develop their capacity to see and appreciate the value of their people. It means internalizing the idea that people are more than tools or talents; that they are individuals who have personal value. As a mentor, the manager enhances the value employees see in themselves and creates an environment in which employees choose to invest themselves in the achievement of organizational goals.

The mentor's role requires the insights, skills, and desire to help others discover their potential. For most, this is not a natural talent, but the necessary insights and skills can be learned. The desire, of course, is more a matter of choice. The most successful companies are recognizing the distinction between managers and mentors and are providing managers who are willing to make this important shift with the opportunity to develop these important skills for success.

In *Daring to Be Different: A Manager's Ascent to Leadership* (2003), Hatherley distinguishes between two types of managers: monarchs and muralists. A monarch typically blocks the full development of those people within his or her sphere of influence. In contrast, muralists are managers who empower themselves and their employees. For managers to be mentors, they must also be leaders. If they are unable to exercise leadership, they risk becoming reverse mentors, demoralizing staff, lowering expectations, and draining the talent pool.

Winthrop Pharmaceuticals

Rotational mentoring

As the twenty-first century opened, Winthrop Pharmaceuticals faced the fact that all of its top-level leaders were going to retire at about the same time. This would happen in four to five years, and there was no one in the pipeline who was capable of moving into a higher-level leadership position.

A previous severe flattening of the organizational pyramid had prevented anyone from moving up, and many potential leaders had not even been able to move laterally. In short, the next generation of future leaders had been plateaued for so long that they were not ready for major promotions to a higher-level positions.

The New York–based company invested in leadership training for its high potential junior staff, but found this insufficient for:

- developing usable competencies,
- gaining practical wisdom, and
- understanding the big picture about emerging market trends and how to be competitive.

Winthrop asked an outside company, Corporate Mentoring Solutions (CMSI), for help. CMSI suggested trying rotational mentoring. Each junior staff with high potential was matched with a top-level mentor for the amount of time required to meet a particular mentee need. Then the mentee rotated to work with another mentor. This rotation continued for three years.

The mentoring program began with a two-day training for the initial mentor-mentee partners. They acquired and applied skills for working together and learned how to use these skills with each new partner. Because everyone learned the same concepts and skills initially, it was much easier for them to transfer this learning to each new partner over the three-year duration of the mentoring program.

Formal evaluation at the 18-month point revealed that mentees were learning specific competencies and getting a big-picture perspective from each new mentor they were matched with.

Mentors were also getting a bigger perspective from each new mentee by finding out what that mentee had done and learned from previous mentors, as well as that mentee's ideas for improving the company in some specific way.

After three years, Winthrop Pharmaceuticals was confident it had developed a pool of future leaders to replace those who were retiring.

MENTORING AND CHANGES IN THE WORKPLACE

Changes attendant to the age of knowledge are making individuals more responsible for their own learning and career development. Concurrently, telecommuting, or flex-place, is on the rise, and freelancing has increased, making it more difficult for people to become part of organizational culture and to acquire knowledge that comes from collaboration with experienced workers. Mentoring appeals to such workers and to organizations that seek to maintain institutional knowledge.

With traditional mentoring, the novice or apprentice learned from a master. In the Industrial Age, mentoring assisted career advancement within organizational hierarchies. Apprenticeships continue today as a feature of many of the trades across Africa. But as the knowledge age ascends, a wide range of cognitive, interpersonal, and technical skills is needed, and mentoring is changing to cope with these expanded needs.[14]

The adoption of formal mentoring programs has occurred rapidly according to Galvin.[15] Of the top 100 companies that excel in human capital development, 77 percent have mentoring programs and believe that mentoring contributes to career development, retention, and leadership succession.

Although formal mentoring programs are growing, informal mentoring relationships still outnumber formal ones. Disney and SunTrust, for example, do not have formal mentoring programs, but many of their employees are in mentoring relationships. Some companies even have junior staff mentor executives, a kind of reverse mentoring. The idea is that younger employees can provide valuable insights, increase performance, and reduce the gap between the generations and even help foster mutuality, clear objectives, respectful interaction, and acceptance of difference.[16]

WHAT DO MENTORS AND MENTEES DO?

Bell likens the mentor's role in experiential learning to that of birds guiding their young in leaving the nest; they support without rescuing, provide scaffolding, and have the courage to let learners fail.[17]

Mentoring is built on a foundation of trust. Mentors provide a safe place for learners to express ideas and to learn new skills and experiment with new roles. When linked with real world activities such as temporary work assignments or short-term projects, this experimentation deepens as a learning experience.[18]

As we have noted, mentoring may be considered a kind of self-directed learning, or mentoring may better enable self-directed learning. In a typical mentoring relationship mentors and mentees:

- talk together (e.g., about the mentor's past experiences; the mentee's goals, plans, and skills; the mentor's career path; useful problem-solving strategies);
- attend meetings and conferences together as joint learning activities;
- work together on activities;
- have the mentee observe the mentor handling challenging situations;
- role-play situations faced by the mentee;
- exchange and discuss written materials (such as a document written by the mentee or an article valued by the mentor);
- interact with other people (including persons who could be of help to the mentee or other mentor-mentee pairs).

A mentor has to make sure that the conversation around continuous development is inspiring, not intimidating. A great leader truly believes that personal development is a never-ending journey. If you can help people embrace and love continuous development, then you are really making a difference in their lives and careers.[19]

Mentoring may include any or all of the following, depending on the needs of mentees and the challenges of the project or organization:

- Being a role model. The mentor demonstrates desired skills, behavior, and attitudes.
- Demonstrating a genuine, personal interest in the welfare and professional growth of mentees.
- Offering suggestions, possibilities, resources, problem-solving approaches, and opportunities to think out loud with mentees regarding current or future issues.
- Providing feedback that is supportive yet frank and accurate and that reinforces success and identifies failure as a learning opportunity.
- Offering motivation directed toward assisting mentees to identify and achieve long-term professional goals.[20]

Inherent to all mentoring approaches is a process of engagement. Unlike the traditional image of the guru, mentees do not learn at the feet of their mentors; rather both mentee and mentor engage in a mutually rewarding learning relationship.

Mentors do a number of very important things that develop individuals, teams, and ultimately the organization and even community. Among their tasks and activities, Ambrose identifies the following:

- Set high performance expectations.
- Offer challenging ideas.
- Help build self-confidence.
- Encourage professional behavior.
- Offer friendship.
- Confront negative behaviors and attitudes.
- Listen to personal problems.
- Teach by example.
- Provide growth experiences.
- Offer quotable quotes.
- Explain how the organization works.
- Help far beyond their duties or obligations.
- Stand by their mentees in critical situations.
- Offer wide counsel.
- Encourage winning behavior.
- Trigger self-awareness.
- Inspire to excellence.
- Share critical knowledge.
- Offer encouragement.
- Assist with careers.[21]

MENTOR AND COACH—SIMILARITIES AND DIFFERENCES

Once especially valuable to project management, mentoring is becoming more important in all areas of the workplace. Mentoring is similar to coaching in some respects because both are processes by which one person (the mentor or coach) assists another person, either formally or informally, in various tasks related to the general purposes of professional growth and development. This assistance often takes the form of guidance and encouragement and may or may not be directly tied to an actual project issue being faced by the individual being assisted. Indeed, coaching and mentoring often become directed at assisting the individual in attaining a broader view of future career direction or advancement.

Differences exist, however. At their core, coaching focuses on performance, whereas mentoring focuses on learning. As Zachary points out, "coaching and mentoring frequently get confused. Coaching is always a part of mentoring, but coaching does not always involve mentoring. Coaching within the context of a mentoring relationship has to do with the skill of helping an individual fill a particular knowledge gap by learning how to do things more effectively."[22]

MATCHING THE MENTOR AND MENTEE

Organizations give a lot of thought to matching mentors and mentees, although some have differences of opinion about the importance of demographics to the matching process. As globalization and organizational diversity increase, the personal relationship at the core of mentoring can be problematic when mentor and mentee are of different genders, races, or ethnic backgrounds. No uniform agreement exists regarding the advantages and disadvantages of matching characteristics in mentoring relationships. Some practitioners recommend matching common background and experience as a way to get mentors and mentees off to a good start. Clearly, mentors need to be sensitive to different cultural perspectives if mentoring is not to contribute to homogeneous, exclusionary values and culture.

Specific demographic issues that receive consideration when matches are considered include the following:

- **Gender.** Women generally have fewer same-sex options for matchups in the mentoring relationship, yet most studies show no sex difference in mentoring preferences. Women do show a slight preference for personal attributes of trustworthiness, integrity, and humanism, whereas men show a slight preference for power, status, and influence in choices of mentors/mentees.[23]

- **Age.** Noe, Rose, Wilde, and Schau all show that older members of a group are somewhat less open to participating in mentoring relationships.[24]

- **Race/ethnicity.** Mentoring among minority and ethnic groups traditionally was seen as a remedy to address discrimination in the workplace and to promote organizational learning and career advancement from which these groups were routinely excluded. Historically, minorities had less access to mentoring programs and fewer opportunities for same-race mentoring. Boreen, Niday, and Hildred show that the dominant culture, with power on its side, can make it difficult for mentors and mentees to work together in trust and openness.[25]

The rapid increase of diversity and the pace of globalization of companies require increasing numbers of managers who are able to function successfully across racial and ethnic groups and in different cultures. The recent proliferation of international executive MBA programs signals this need and points up the work that traditional business schools have to do to adapt their programs to the reality of globalization.

Mentees who may have choices among mentors should consider the following:

1. In very small organizations a manager may mentor his or her own staff, but normally a manager in another department should be sought. Managers find it especially hard to function effectively as an objective mentor for their own staffs.
2. Other senior people within your company who have followed similar career paths may be a good choice. Mentors may also be found in partner companies or affiliates, though corporate competitors should be avoided. Professional associations are a good way to meet top people in one's field.
3. A manager with similar values, work style, and sense of humor or someone whom you admire or whom you find uplifting may be a good choice.

COST

Mentoring requires some investment in selecting mentors, matching mentors and mentees, and in training mentors. But this must be set against the potential it has for retaining employees and for supporting creativity in the workplace.

The most significant costs involved are those related to administering the training of mentors. Many firms find it an expensive affair to bring all the employees together for a mentoring program. But as mentoring programs have achieved the status in many organizations as a way to gain competitive advantage through people development, focus has gathered on cost saving to this investment. Many companies, for example, have discovered that the use of a mentor for new employees not only helps employees settle into their job and company environment but also contributes to a lower turnover rate.[26]

GROWING IMPORTANCE OF MENTORING

Mentoring has been growing as an important issue in management theory and practice over the past 25 years as the need for continuous learning and systems thinking have become critical for the survival of organizations. Mentoring, as we have shown in this chapter, must be adapted to the learning needs of adults as well as the new trends in the workplace, such as virtual mentoring and cross-cultural mentoring. Mentoring models including communities of practice and action learning increasingly are being employed to address the mentoring issues of learning, leadership development, career development, retention, and the matching of mentor and mentee.

THREE

New Roles and Responsibilities for the Mentor

GROWING IMPORTANCE OF MENTORING

Mentoring is becoming more important in both private and public sectors. Some companies are reducing the staff of internal training departments and shifting employee development functions to department leaders or project managers. Today's technical employee, working in a robust economy, expects that value-added benefits, such as coaching and mentoring, will be available within the workplace.

Managers who take on roles as mentors find themselves responsible for their employees in ways that were not part of traditional management models. They become responsible for employees' development, growth, and well-being. They find themselves being sometime ally, coach, and catalyst and wear the hats of teacher, advisor, planner, pathfinder, protector, supporter, role model, tactician, and storyteller.[1]

This chapter will look at the activities and style of the mentor; services the mentor provides; the mentor's key roles of change agent, listener, and questioner; and the fundamental services of career development and psychological support that mentors provide. This chapter will focus on the phases of mentoring—preparing, negotiating, enabling, and closure—wherein mentors play secondary roles of evaluator, strategist/stimulator, and catalyst/facilitator. An in-depth look at the mentor's responsibility for providing feedback will highlight the importance of questioning and listening. Finally, this chapter considers why mentoring programs and relationships may fail and the ways to approach failing relationships.

General George Marshall, chief of staff during World War II, President Truman's secretary of state from 1947 to 1948 and secretary of defense from 1950 to 1952, was one of Dwight D. Eisenhower's most important mentors. As chief of staff, he was responsible for Eisenhower's meteoric rise during World War II. He was the man from whom Eisenhower sought advice, counsel, and approval. Eisenhower said that of all the Americans he knew, "George Marshall possessed more of the qualities of greatness than has any other."

ACTIVITIES AND STYLE OF THE MENTOR

Mentor activities and behaviors may include any or all of the following, depending on the needs of the mentee:

- **Being role models,** demonstrating desired skills, behavior, and attitudes whose adoption may benefit mentees.
- **Demonstrating genuine, personal interest** in the welfare and professional growth of mentees.
- **Offering suggestions, possibilities, resources, problem-solving approaches, and opportunities** to think out loud with the mentees regarding current or future issues.
- **Providing feedback that is supportive yet frank and accurate** to reinforce successes and portray failures as learning opportunities.
- **Offering motivation** to assisting mentees in identifying and achieving long-term professional goals.

Although mentees may be intensely involved in projects, the mentoring relationship allows the mentee to step away from production issues and focus on learning issues. The mentor may help the mentee see how to approach a problem or issue differently in the future.

A mentoring relationship is often best suited to a project manager and a mentee on another team. Such a relationship often allows both parties to focus more clearly on the developmental needs of the mentee, free of distractions that can occur when both parties are working on the same team.

Many organizations that sponsor mentoring programs stipulate that a mentoring relationship should be between professionals who do not work with each other.

The style or tone of a mentoring relationship is something that should be presented with caution. For example, some mentees may find a mentor who is parental in style to be calming and reassuring; others might find it irritating, even insulting. Some people prefer a mentor whose tone is like a big sister; still others might prefer a mentor whose tone suggests that the mentor and mentee are two equals drawn together by the goal of solving specific problems. This tone suggests both partners are capable of leading the process of crafting the solution.

What tone does the mentor want to set and what style does she want to offer? Is it a style the mentee will respond well to? The parties must discuss these style questions before they agree to a mentoring relationship. Like any relationship, this discussion needs to examine honestly what each party wants for the relationship and what each party is capable of giving.

CAREER DEVELOPMENT AND PSYCHOLOGICAL SUPPORT—THE TWO KEY SERVICES OF MENTORING

Career Development for Mentor and Mentee

Successful mentoring programs provide clear benefits for all participants. Mentees customize the learning agenda and gain greater control over their careers. They get access to, and advice from, senior-level managers as well as exposure to other functional areas and opportunities. Mentees can also take advantage of real-time learning and development instead of waiting for scheduled classroom programs. Mentors increase their managerial and leadership skills. Older mentors get new business perspectives and insight from younger mentees. Reverse mentoring (younger mentors/older mentees) produces the same gains.

The following statistics come from various national surveys, all conducted between 1995 and 2004:

- When executives of Fortune 500 companies were surveyed, 96 percent said mentoring is an important developmental tool, and 75 percent said it played a key role in their personal career success.
- Of Fortune 500 and private companies, 71 percent use mentoring in their organizations.
- In a survey of U.S. companies with formal mentoring programs, 77 percent indicated that mentoring improved both retention and performance of employees.

- Employees who have had mentors earn between $5,610 and $22,450 more per year than employees who have not had mentors.
- A survey of college and graduate students showed that 60 percent said mentoring is a factor they will consider when selecting a job after graduation.[2]

Psychological Support

For many workers, the assistance provided by a mentor trained in listening skills will be the most effective part of the mentor/mentee relationship. Mentor/mentee relationships that are founded on caring, mutual respect, and active listening and have qualities of effective helping, trust, sincerity, nonjudgment, and positive regard will be the most effective in assisting mentees to explore their problems or concerns and will lead to greater personal growth and development.

In their psychosocial roles, mentors act as role models and counselors, offering confirmation, clarification, and emotional support. An important psychosocial role for mentors is to help the mentee understand and resolve issues mentees encounter in their sometimes contradictory world inside and outside of the workplace.

"My mentee is really in a funk since his father died. Things had been going so well, but now he seems distracted and just goes through the motions."

"Gee, Wendy, you have had a number of barriers in this relationship," said Wayne.

"I talked with our mentoring coordinator. She suggested laying out options. We could suspend the mentoring and pick it up later; we could include the impact of his father's death in our relationship; or Karl could take advantage of the counseling center our company refers to. He wants to keep going."

"Well your relationship is probably a steadying force for him tight now."

"Yes, I think so," said Wendy. "We'll see. By the way, I am going to start some team mentoring when this relationship is concluded."

"What?"

"Yes, there will be six mentees. I really am going to rely on peer mentoring in three groups of two and we will all meet together once every two weeks. By the way, how is your relationship going after, what, 12 weeks, now?"

"Well, we have 3 more weeks, and it has been great. At first I thought I couldn't wait to get through the 15 weeks, but now I think I will miss these meetings."

"Good, you can sign up for another mentee," replied Wendy.

"I suppose. You know, yesterday Jocelyn asked a question so profound that we could only stare at each other for about 15 seconds. Finally I said, 'That was one of the best questions I have ever heard. Maybe we are closer to closure than I thought.' We both had a good laugh."

Mentoring is not the same as psychological counseling, but the mentor's approach is analogous to the psychologist's, in that the mentor encourages the mentee to discover his learning needs, remove the blocks to these needs, and pursue a healthy (successful) path toward meeting these needs. Mentoring, like action learning, draws upon a number of disciplines, including psychology and sociology, and thus the language that describes the mentor's facilitating role may sound familiar to the counselor. For example:

- The mentor helps the mentee identify real issues, not just symptoms or manifestations of problems.
- The mentor is interested both in issue resolution and in the learning value of the process for the mentee.
- When the mentee has identified a real issue, the mentor helps investigate its causes and listens closely to the mentee's feelings about the issue.
- The mentor is prepared for the mentee's complicating the problem, either through faulty judgment, confused thinking, or by avoiding the work of confronting the situation.
- Once the mentee has taken responsibility for the issue and its resolution, the mentor encourages action.
- The mentor pushes the mentee toward action by asking direct and penetrating questions.

A good mentor is a person who has experienced nurturing and is willing to help connect with a person. They must be knowledgeable and understand that eventually the mentee becomes a peer. The letting go part can be difficult, but at some point, the mentor has to stand back and let go.

—Donna Gilton, associate professor, Graduate School of Library and Information Studies, University of Rhode Island

The mentor may make suggestions and offer advice but never in place of empowering the mentee to take charge of his own analysis and decision-making processes. The mentee should feel both comfortable and confident in developing his or her own ideas and action plans before the mentor offers suggestions. Ideally, the mentor remains in the mode of inquiry, gently but persistently questioning the ideas, decisions, and learning of the mentee.

THE ROLES OF THE MENTOR

The mentor plays many roles depending on the needs of the mentee and the phase of the mentoring relationship. The most important of these are change agent, listener, and questioner. These broad roles, played successfully, enable the mentor to become ally, catalyst, strategist, counselor, cheerleader, teacher, advisor, pathfinder, protector, role model, and storyteller.

Change Agent

Today's manager must be a different breed. Traditionally, managers were concerned with transactions, reporting, and control. In the knowledge age, however, managers must be leaders, build relationships, and bring fresh insight and experience to day-to-day challenges. Managers today must be agents of change.

David Maister offers a number of qualities that successful managers, as change agents, must exhibit, according to a survey of workers from around the world.[3] The list includes such characteristics as: apolitical, accessible all the time, articulate about what you stand for, comfortable with allowing others to get credit, good at reading people's character and skill level, sensitive to personal issues, smart but human, unquestionably honest, and disciplined about standards yet open to reasons why they may not be met.

Managers must be flexible enough to communicate up, down, and across organizations. They need to take a comprehensive approach in day-to-day decision making. They must be strategic planners, able to see the long-term implications and significance of what they are doing.

As agents of change managers must be able to see, grasp, and facilitate opportunities for innovation and collaboration. They must be able to bring people together. In learning and empowering organizations, the following behavioral characteristics describe equally well the manager and the mentor. According to Seldin, the mentor:

- Builds upon the individual's experience and knowledge. She knows and makes the most of the strengths and abilities of her mentee.
- Extends the freedom to risk and make mistakes. When he encourages this freedom, his mentee is motivated to be curious and innovative.

- Entertains multiple options; more than one "right way." Openness to diversity boosts the mentee's feelings that what he has contributed is valued.
- Appeals to the mentee's creativity and desire to grow personally.
- Uses open-ended questions that promote discovery of new possibilities. An open-ended, problem-solving attitude helps the mentee to deal with new issues and to embrace the testing and acceptance/rejection of hypotheses.
- Models unconditionally constructive communication. The mentor/manager should model healthy communication, eschewing gossip or disrespectful references to others.
- Demonstrates mutual respect. Mentees will imitate the modeling of respectful treatment.
- Shows her willingness to influence and be influenced. Learning is dynamic, and mentors, as well as mentees, should be in the learning mode.
- Minimizes differences in power and status. The manager/mentor does not abdicate his responsibility of leadership but treats the mentee in a fashion that does not imply an "above" or "below" position.
- Demonstrates interest in the success of the mentee.
- Expresses empathy for people's challenges, fears, and personal obstacles.
- Avoids posturing and defensiveness. Mentees will adopt negative as well as positive behavior modeled by the mentor.
- Gives full attention to how the mentee is behaving as well as what he is doing.[4]

Listener

Among the most important roles of the mentor that give shape to all others is that of listener. Listening enables the mentor to understand the developmental needs of the mentee. Empathetic listening will help guide the mentee to a response appropriate to the mentee's current development need.

A mentor also needs a strong sense of self—including being a good listener— and a willingness to be vulnerable and open to irreducible differences and to meeting those differences and engaging them; an openness to being surprised in what happens in the encounter in interpersonal relationships.

—David Ames, Episcopal chaplain at Brown University

Skillful, effective listening is at the core of the following characteristics that mark successful managers and mentors:

- **Vision:** The visionary leader, manager, or mentor listens to the values held by her employees, or mentees, and links organizational goals to their long-term goals.
- **Delegation:** The effective manager/leader/mentor listens to employees, establishes personal rapport and trust, and helps them to understand how their performance matters. Delegation of decision-making authority to the employee within his area of responsibility—including the power to make and learn from mistakes—is crucial to the effectiveness of today's leader. This style of leadership accelerates innovation and learning at all levels of the organization.
- **Democracy:** The democratic manager/leader/mentor elicits fresh ideas by listening carefully to opinions and information of employees/mentees. Goleman, McKee, and Boyatzis contrast this behavior to that of managers who manage by objectives, setting ambitious goals and monitoring progress toward those goals, including the behavior of their employees.[5] These managers do not have the same need for listening because the course has been predetermined and everyone should be on board. In such situations, managers are more likely to issue instructions without asking for input about what is to be done.

Mentors try to unite the head and the heart, coming across and being a whole person, being a good listener. The word "education" literally means "drawing out from" rather than filling up. If you get away from the power relationship, the more you can grow, and the more you can give back in return.

—Art Stein, professor of political science,
University of Rhode Island

Questioner

Questioning is the second of the two most important roles of the mentor, those around which all other roles revolve. Questions, especially challenging ones, cause us to think and to learn. Questions create energy and vitality in the mentoring partnership because they trigger a need to listen, to seek a common truth, and to justify opinions and viewpoints. Questions generate a dialogue in which people begin to leave their individual limitations to find a new wholeness.[6] Shared inquiry transforms the mentor/mentee relationship into an opportunity to experiment with ideas and test new abilities in a constructive atmosphere.

Thomas MacAvoy, former CEO of Corning Glass, relates that the most creative question he ever asked was put to his chief chemist: "Glass breaks. Why don't you do something about that?" This resulted in 25 different ways of preventing glass from breaking. Eighteen of them worked, and five made money for the company.[7]

When looking for ideas, the first step is often asking great questions, because the way we look at the problem can dictate how we seek its solution. In creative problem solving, it is more important to ask the right questions than to give the right answers. If managers ask the wrong questions, all the right answers are of little use.

When someone goes off track, asking a direct question like, "Is that what you really meant?" or "Is this going where you had intended?" is a great way to help regain the original path. Questions help mentees find answers for themselves, help create self-esteem, and empower them to do more for themselves. Questions are important to the mentees; they learn to ask good questions by hearing good questions and receiving feedback on the questions they pose. The asking of questions turns mentees into self-motivated learners.

Questions can be particularly helpful in group mentoring situations. Asking the group "How can we solve this together?" can turn potential conflict into a teamwork situation. Mentees will realize they do not have to deal with the situation alone.

Through careful questioning, mentors give mentees the opportunity to explain themselves. Responses relate to the type of questions asked, and it is important to frame the question to enable a suitable and relevant answer.

Questioner is the most important role a mentor can have. Questioning encourages strategy development, it challenges and stimulates, it empowers the mentee with options in action, it encourages reflection, and subsequently it deepens learning in the mentee. When the mentor asks questions, and refrains from supplying the mentee with answers, it dramatically changes the mentee's experience.

Ambrose (1998) identifies three types of questioning, each with its specific objectives:[8]

Investigation. Investigative questions establish facts and objective data and tend to establish a historical progression in which the past enlightens the present. These are the *what, when, who, why,* and *where* questions. Examples of investigative questions may include:

- When did your interest in this project develop?
- How long have you worked on this activity or program?

- What have you accomplished so far in this project?
- With whom have you collaborated in these activities?

Discovery. These questions are often reflective and encourage the mentee to learn from experiences and gain new insight or knowledge. Examples of discovery questions include:

- What have your learned from this experience?
- What are you learning about yourself?
- What are the choices available to you?
- What has been the impact of the choices you have made so far?

Empowerment. These questions both imply and invest power in the mentee to accomplish her goals. They probe the mentee's desires, plans, and level of commitment. Examples of empowerment questions include:

- What do you want to happen?
- How will you put your plan into action?
- What will you do first?
- How will you use the resources available to you?

The best questions will be those that promote growth and development of the mentee. The mentor must take care not to become enamored of his questions nor to provide answers on the mentee's behalf. The questioning mode will push mentees to examine the issues and their motives. Mentors must resist their own problem-solving orientation and allow mentees to examine their own thinking processes.

Mentors should be prepared when mentees seek suggestions. Although the inquiry process is a powerful learning tool to stimulate and empower the mentee, mentees also learn from the mentor's experience and suggestions. The mentor may want to take care that the mentee has had ample opportunity to reflect on his own thoughts and ideas before offering suggestions.[9]

THE PHASES OF MENTORING

Zachary shows that mentoring relationships progress through four phases: preparing, negotiating, enabling, and coming to closure.[10] Mentors and mentees play out their roles as they move through these stages in a spiral progression. Regular reflection throughout these stages empowers, informs, enlightens, and strengthens the mentor's facilitation role and maximizes the learning of the mentee throughout each. Omission of these phases is likely to result in dissatisfaction for both parties in the relationship.

Preparation

Mentors must be realistic in their assessment of their commitment. Mentoring is not an occasion for assessing whether one's resume will benefit but whether one can make the investment appropriate to the mentee's needs. Mentors must assess their capability to mentor and simultaneously identify opportunities for learning and self-development. Both mentor and mentee evaluate the viability of the prospective relationship.[11] (See chapter 7 for tools to help assess mentor readiness.)

During the preparation phase mentors may ask mentees to assess themselves, to identify their strengths and areas they need to work on. They should also probe the mentees' short-term and long-term goals. These will help make the negotiation phase realistic.

During preparation, mentors also divulge their expectations of the relationship. If the manager/mentor has no personal goals for the relationship, it will be difficult for him to sustain the interest and energy required to carry it to closure. Mentoring relationships should be mutual; both partners should benefit, even as the focus is on the learning needs of the mentee. Both partners should be prepared for an honest discussion of expectations of each other during the preparation phase. Otherwise they risk resentment and recrimination at a later point in the mentoring relationship.[12]

All mentors should make sure that their enthusiasm, willingness, and desire are balanced by a realistic assessment before they commit to mentoring. They should consider the prospective mentee's background and other relevant information to assure there is a fit, and they should be clear that mentoring will require an investment of time, depending on the mentee's goals and needs.[13]

Negotiation

Here the mentor and mentee establish the terms and conditions of the relationship. They set goals and agree on the content and process of the relationship. The mentor and mentee should aim for a mutual understanding about their assumptions, expectations, goals, and needs. They should also address issues such as confidentiality, boundaries, and limits. If they fail to address these issues through discomfort or neglect, the relationship may never achieve its potential, and both will be disappointed.[14]

During the negotiating phase, much of the mentor/mentee focus is evaluative. The mentor helps identify the strengths and weaknesses of the mentee in order to set short-term training and longer-term development needs. The mentor's aim is to assist the mentee in self-analysis with respect to achievement of long-term goals. Some ways that mentors can be helpful during this evaluation process include:

- Ask mentees to assess their strengths and weaknesses.
- Clarify mentees' short- and long-term goals.
- Share their expectations of the relationship.
- Invite frank discussion of mutual expectations for the relationship.
- Agree on clear and reasonable objectives for the partnership.
- Determine the logistics for the partnership.

Mentoring partners can benefit from a written agreement, contract, or covenant, developed during the negotiation phase. This agreement can be modified during the course of the relationship, and it should guide the activities of the partners and may include the following items:

- short- and long-term objectives of the relationship,
- mentee learning goals,
- expectations of both partners for the relationship,
- contributions both must make to the relationship,
- a schedule of formal meetings,
- procedures for managing informal contact,
- an agenda for the first planned session,
- an agreement about confidentiality, and
- a stipulation of the role as mentor as distinct from the role of the mentee's manager.[15]

The mentor's behavior in the negotiation phase should help the mentee to move forward toward the heart of the relationship. During this phase the mentor models some of the very behavior that will characterize the enabling phase of the relationship.

Enabling

Enabling is the implementation phase of the mentorship and consumes most of the participants' time. This phase builds on the mutual understanding previously established. In this phase the partners focus on the mentee's learning needs. The mentor nurtures the mentee's learning by establishing and maintaining an open and affirming learning climate and providing thoughtful, timely, candid, and constructive feedback. Both participants monitor the mentee's learning goals to ensure they are being met.[16]

In this phase, the mentor's secondary roles as ally, catalyst, and strategist are particularly evident. The mentor's role as an ally implies the development of trust. Trust is the most important part of the relationship and is especially crucial at the beginning. The mentee is unlikely to share his innermost desires, uncertainties, and dreams except in an environment of confidence and trust.

As catalyst the mentor leads the mentee into unfamiliar territory (new people, situations, and challenges) and sees what takes place. The mentee's response to the new and unexpected will help him to reflect on his capabilities and to stretch his development goals.

Walt Whitman once wrote, "I contain a multitude." Mentors need to nurture the multitude in all of us.

—Scott Holland, pastor, Monroeville
Church of the Brethren, Monroeville, Pennsylvania

As coach or strategist, the mentor helps select and organize experiences for growth and learning. The partners should discuss long-term development goals, consider work assignments or experiences aimed at fulfilling those aims, and track their progress. Mentors should facilitate new development, seek excellence, and help mentees surpass themselves.[17]

Zachary lists a number of ways to support mentees in the enabling phase.[18] These include:

- Meet on a regular basis.
- Expect the relationship to take time to develop.
- Be consistent in your participation.
- From time to time, revisit the expectations of all parties in the relationship.
- Monitor the relationship to make sure that it is objective driven.
- Anticipate the need for midcourse corrections.
- Periodically evaluate the relationship against its learning goals.
- Maintain openness to learning opportunities.
- Give the relationship space.
- Provide regular feedback to your mentoring partner.

These processes lie at the heart of the relationship and continue until the mentee's learning goals have been achieved. As part of the enabling process the mentor stimulates and motivates self-development in the mentee. The mentor does this by asking questions, listening actively, challenging assumptions, offering encouragement, and avoiding assumptions or decision making for the mentee. The mentor's questions will help the mentee to focus on the real issues at hand. Once these are clear, they can jointly examine feelings about the issue and resolve blocks to its resolution. During this process, the mentor focuses equally on the learning process of the mentee.[19]

During the enabling phase the mentor assists the mentee to access learning opportunities and to connect him with resources within and without the organization. The mentor should refrain from drawing attention to his influence or connections during this process and should not claim credit for the mentee's success or progress.

The mentor encourages the mentee to act on his issues or learning goals in this phase. When the mentee has identified issues and potential choices, the mentor encourages the mentee to take responsibility, through action, for issue resolution.

Within each of us is an ecology of self voices. We each have the capacity to birth a voice that is authentically one's own and that works within one's profession. Mentors can be helpful in drawing forth that voice. It's not about parroting. It's not social reproduction.

—James Keen, professor of social and global studies,
Antioch College

The mentor's job is to facilitate growth and development and the problem-solving capacity of the mentee. Mentors should, as a rule, refrain from giving advice or answering every question the mentee poses. The mentee will improve her ability to frame the issue appropriately as long as the mentor does not do this for her. Rather, the mentor's task is, through probing with investigative and discovery questions, to help the mentee gain clarity on the issue before her.[20]

As part of the mentee's learning journey, a manager/mentor may introduce the mentee to other managers. This will help the mentee to broaden her career horizons while introducing other managers to new talent.

Feedback

Giving feedback is critical to the mentee's progress and to the success of the enabling process and is one of the more delicate roles a mentor plays. Feedback is dependent on effective questioning and listening skills and lays out to the mentee what he has been saying and implying, the direction of his learning, and the correspondence of his learning and actions.

Feedback is one of the mentor's most valuable gifts to the mentee. Feedback may be corrective or confirming, but it must always be honest. Honest, constructive feedback can free and encourage the mentee to grow in competence and confidence and enrich his learning. Feedback helps the mentoring partners to overcome obstacles to learning and is critical to the enabling process.

Giving and receiving of feedback are considered to be core managerial skills. Within the context of mentoring they take on particular significance because the mentor's views are often seen as carrying additional impact. This stems from the status and expertise of the mentor or his position as an impartial observer. Consequently it is vital for mentors to be able to offer feedback in such a way mentees not only receive it but welcome it.

Feedback to mentees needs to be both honest and positive. In terms of honesty mentors should never say anything they know to be untrue. Mentors should focus first on mentees' strengths, and emphasize them, before turning to the weaknesses. In addressing weaknesses it is important to investigate how each can be dealt with by the mentee and what role the mentor can play. This is an example of positive feedback to address weaknesses.

Similarly, receiving feedback is a skill that has to be developed. From the mentor's point of view it is important in two aspects. First, receiving feedback positively from the mentee will improve the relationship, and second, as a result, mentors, as role models, will be better able to guide mentees in the receipt of feedback.

Although honest feedback can be helpful to mentees, mentors should be prepared for resistance and denial. A mentee in denial may appear to be surprised, even shocked, at the mentor's feedback. The mentor can assist the mentee to work through resistance and denial by providing information that links past conversations to present issues.

Mentees who resist feedback may doubt their abilities, feel hurt, or blame others for their troubles. Letting mentees vent before offering suggestions can be helpful. Sometimes venting can benefit from the cooler time between meetings.

Mentees are reenergized by feedback, especially when it is specific, explicit, and timely. Some individuals appear to have boundless energy once they receive feedback. After giving feedback, mentors can be helpful by focusing the mentees on priority setting so that they can identify new courses of action and consider new possibilities.

The ultimate goal of feedback is to redirect the mentee's action and learning. Feedback can help a mentee to move forward to meet new challenges. It offers an opportunity for reflection in action and may help the mentee develop an action plan and become comfortable with follow-up and accountability mechanisms. The first successful feedback event will pave the way for a series of others during the course of the mentoring partnership and will provide the mentee both skill and courage in providing appropriate feedback of his own.

A mentor must be careful to protect the mentee's pride and sense of self by avoiding giving feedback in too judgmental a manner. In fact, feedback can be a dialogue. The mentor may approach feedback as a process of discovery by asking the mentee for some self-assessment and by listening carefully before reacting to the mentee's self-appraisal.

When giving feedback, mentors, in addition to being specific, should remember to emphasize learning, to be prepared to discuss alternative courses of action, and to offer help, as appropriate.[21]

Dealing with Obstacles

During the enabling phase, the mentor is liable to encounter a number of obstacles. Every partnership faces obstacles at one time or another. These may be personal, related to the mentee's experience, belief systems, or biases; or organizational, related to the mentee's work situation, understanding of his job, or career plans. Mentors support, challenge, and offer to facilitate mentees' growth and development, despite the obstacles they face. Mentors should not underestimate the presence or the power of obstacles to mentoring relationships and should attempt to anticipate problems that can undermine productive relationships.

Some obstacles may originate with the mentee. The mentee may be unfocused, seemingly unable to follow through. He may be manipulative and seek to control the relationship without committing to the hard work of self-assessment and learning. He may display apathy, showing energy only when seeking immediate gratification. Mentors must be prepared to challenge and encourage mentees who present obstacles by bringing them back to the mentoring agreement, revisiting goals and strategies, and examining the consequences of their behavior.

Mentees may become overly dependent on mentors, expecting them to provide answers or even become responsible for learning strategies. Mentors must resist rescuing mentees or solving their problems. Rather, they should put mentees' behavior in the spotlight, making it an issue to examine and reflect upon. The mentor might even recall similar dependency strategies in his own career and share their futility with the mentee.

Other obstacles originate with mentors. Mentors may saddle themselves with the notion that they must meet all their mentees' needs. They may have race, gender, or age biases that influence the relationship in subtle, but negative, ways. They may experience stress that distracts them from clear focus on the relationship. Mentors must provide themselves feedback by reflecting on the notes of their meetings with mentors and on their behavior and comments during the meeting. They should also invite and take seriously mentee feedback.

"This has not been a good day," Wayne lamented.

"What happened?" asked Wendy.

"During our meeting today, I made a negative comment about one of our presidential candidates. Jocelyn looked startled. I went on quickly, as though it hadn't happened. I can't believe I did that!"

"Hmm, why not call her at work tomorrow and tell her you regret your mistake and that if she supports that candidate, your judgmental comments do not extend to her. Look, we have all been tense over this election. As mature as she seems, I think she will understand."

"I just can't believe I made such a dumb mistake," Wayne went on.

"Mentoring relationships are partnerships, Wayne, of people who are not perfect, who can learn from each other, and who can boost each other's learning when they take risks, admit mistakes and vulnerability, and stay as honest as they can."

Wayne looked at Wendy for several seconds. "You're right," he said. "I'll call Jocelyn in the morning."

Jealousy can become an obstacle for both mentor and mentee. The mentor may become jealous of the mentee's progress, imagining the mentee will become more successful and recognized than himself. The mentee may become jealous of his own progress and insights and perceive the mentor as holding him back, even subverting his progress.

Normally, these obstacles can be overcome with openness, honest feedback, and recognition that both partners determine their own learning goals. On the occasion that an obstacle cannot be overcome by the two parties, they may seek assistance from the mentoring coordinator, or it may be a sign that the mentoring relationship should be concluded.[22]

CLOSURE

All mentoring relationships come to an end. When the ending is planned and its potential impact understood, it will benefit both partners. Closure identifies and celebrates accomplishments of the mentee and the benefits of the relationship to both partners.

Closure is anticipated as early as the negotiating phase, when the mentoring partners establish a schedule in their partnership agreement. Closure is a short, well-defined process that offers opportunity for growth and reflection even if the relationship has not met expectations.

Coming to closure presents a challenge to mentoring partners for many reasons. First, relationships can end earlier or last longer than anticipated in the agreement. Sometimes partners are reluctant to let go of a relationship that has provided comfort and affirmation, even though learning goals have been achieved.

Second, closure always elicits emotional responses from the partners. Although acknowledging that discomfort, anxiety, fear, disappointment, relief, and joy are part of a healthy relationship, dealing with these emotions takes more time than many mentors and mentees anticipate.

If neither mentor nor mentee has experienced closure of an intense relationship, they may find themselves adrift. They may have become friends and fear closure will harm the friendship. Closure needs to take place, however, and drawing out closure serves neither partner well.

Closure should mark a transition between what has been learned and accomplished and the postmentoring phase, which may or may not involve a continuing relationship. Sometimes relationships end before their planned time. Even a healthy relationship can end prematurely because of personal circumstances extrinsic to the mentor and mentee. In such an instance, prior planning about dealing with unanticipated obstacles will have helped mentoring partners know how to proceed.

Despite prior planning, knowing when the time for closure has come can be difficult. Usually there are clear signals, such as the successful accomplishment of learning goals. But sometimes the signs may not be so clear.

Coming to closure challenges both mentoring partners. The termination of a mentoring relationship can engender anxiety, resentment, or surprise, and these emotions can cloud the positive accomplishments of both mentor and mentee. Sometimes the relationship continues simply because neither partner wants to face the difficult emotions and loss of personal ties that may accompany closure. Sometimes inertia or a sense of comfort sustains a mentoring relationship long after it should otherwise end. In a planned mentoring program, a specific end date for the program cycle usually dictates when the relationship should end. The result is that partners sometimes stay in mentoring relationships even though the learning goals have been achieved, or they conclude on time but without having achieved learning goals.

Mentor and mentee should first anticipate closure when the mentoring partnership agreement is negotiated. The ending date may be flexible and be based upon the achievement of learning goals. This places responsibility on both partners to monitor progress toward these goals and to recognize when closure is appropriate.

Mentee goals and the progress toward their achievement can be the signal of the immanence of closure. When goals and objectives have been met, partners may chose to establish new goals and renegotiate the terms of engagement. Otherwise, the time for closure has arrived.

Without closure, neither mentor not mentee will adequately reflect on the learning that has taken place, nor will they incorporate and integrate what has been learned as a result of the relationship. Closure provides the mentor with a final opportunity to help a mentee evaluate learning outcomes and identify how to maximize and build on that learning.[23]

Closure should include some formal celebration that is planned by both partners. This may be a luncheon with other mentoring partners where mentors and mentees share with one another their accomplishments and the impact of mentoring on their future.

The closure of successful relationships may not be the end of the mentor/mentee relationship. The mentee may consider the mentor a confidant and report his progress at various stages of his career. Mentors should be prepared to provide continuing positive feedback to mentees on occasion long after the relationship has reached closure.

WHEN RELATIONSHIPS FAIL

Sometimes the mentoring partnership and/or the mentoring program fail. Understanding the causes of failure can be a key to ensuring success. Mentoring programs and relationships may fail for a variety of reasons. According to Clutterbuck, these may be:

- **Contextual.** Program failures may result from a lack of clarity of purpose or lack of support within the organizational culture. Relationships, too, can fail when purpose, expectations, or mentoring styles are unclear. If the purpose is unclear then the role of mentoring in achieving the partners' goals will not be clear, and the relationship will fade away within a short time. Managers and mentors need to know why the mentoring program has been instituted, what is expected of the partners, what are the respective roles and responsibilities of mentor and mentee, and what are the desired outcomes. Clarity of purpose can energize the relationship. Clear goals and purposes will result in more focused discussions and an ease of relating meeting agendas to the mentee's larger goals. Mentoring must receive consistent support from within the organization. If mentors and mentees are penalized for taking working time out for their meetings, then their efforts will falter.
- **Interpersonal.** Interpersonal problems may also be internal or external to the relationship. If the mentee's unit manager does not understand or support the goals of the mentoring program, he may, through jealousy or intimidation, subvert the relationship by putting conflicting demands on the mentee and making it difficult for her to keep her commitment. Mentees' managers should be involved in the mentoring program, especially in its design and evaluation, as a way of ensuring their understanding and support. They should realize that any issues the mentees may raise about them or their management styles will remain confidential in the mentoring partnership. Resentment may arise from people who are not included in common, especially with regard to cross-gender

pairs. Openness about the program and why it targets particular groups of people helps to overcome misconceptions.

- **Procedural.** Procedural problems relate to the management of the program or relationship. At the program level, mentoring can be overmanaged. Program designers may provide, for example, explicit instructions about how to proceed, what to talk about, or how to evaluate. Such behavior can stifle spontaneity and individual focus of effective mentoring. At the other extreme the sponsoring office may offer too little direction, with little provision to support the mentoring partners when they run into difficulty or when they need advice. Among mentoring relationships, mentors sometimes fail to find an appropriate balance between being direct and indirect. Knowing when to lead and when to let the mentee take the lead is an important mentoring skill.[24]

Again, according to Clutterbuck, as many as 40 percent of mentoring programs and relationships do not meet one or more of the following criteria:

- achievement of a clear business purpose (e.g., improving retention in a target group of mentees by 25 percent or more),
- achievement of most mentees' personal development objectives,
- learning by most of the mentors, and
- willingness of both parties to engage in mentoring (as mentor or mentee).

Signals let partners know that the relationship is failing. These may include:

- boredom or lack of interest,
- failure to keep an agenda,
- resentment of the time and energy required to maintain the relationship,
- overdependence of the mentee,
- frequent breach of confidence,
- lack of follow through by either party,
- lack of progress over a long time, and
- unpleasant encounters.

These may be signals of lack of commitment, mismatch of mentor and mentee, lack of respect, or lack of readiness for a mentoring relationship. Under any of these circumstances, if either party indicates an intention to end the relationship, the other should respect these wishes.[25]

If the mentoring relationship is ending for any of the reasons cited previously, the mentoring partners may still gain valuable learning if:

1. they do not recriminate or pass judgment for the failure,
2. they take time to consider what went right with the relationship as well as what went wrong and apply that learning to their work situation,
3. they acknowledge the progress and accomplishments that did result from the relationship.

MAKING THE RELATIONSHIP MEANINGFUL

Both the mentor and the mentee bear responsibility for a meaningful mentoring relationship. Here are some guidelines to help the relationship be productive:

- Define your relationship mutually, including expectations and responsibilities of both parties and length and frequency of meetings, then stay within these parameters.
- Respect each other's time. Except in unusual circumstances, save questions and ideas for scheduled meetings.
- Both parties should keep a notebook and record questions, action plans, items for discussion, and meeting notes.
- Both should strive to remain open-minded. Feedback should be taken in the spirit it is given.

"You know, Wayne, with Karl I think I have finally achieved a relationship of mutuality. We are honest and respect each other, and we really have learned a lot from each other. If you remember, I had my doubts about Karl at first."

"I think when you gave him power over the relationship, that was the turning point, Wendy."

"Yes, I think it was. By the way, how did your senior staff meeting go? Did you bring your mentee?"

"Yes, her brief presentation and the way she handled herself were fantastic! I gave her lots of praise afterward. But what really amazed me was that my stature seemed to grow by bringing her. A couple of members, more senior than I, called me to say what a great job I had done. It's as though by empowering someone else, I have become more powerful, more successful myself."

Managers who serve as mentors have traditionally provided two key services to their mentees: career development and psychosocial support. Additional ways in which mentors can serve their mentees and the organization at large include mentoring in groups, mentoring virtually, and mentoring for organizational change. Chapter 3 explored each of these traditional and new roles and described how to most effectively carry out each of those roles.

FOUR

Values and Skills of the Mentor

Chapter 1 described how leadership and management are merging in a world of work that is becoming more open, flexible, virtual, diverse, and dependent upon constant learning. Advances in information technology, and the process of globalization that has emerged from these advances, have caused cultural upheavals that impact every major institution in every nation of the globe. Mentors can stimulate and facilitate the learning needed by workers in modern organizations and can guide mentees through these confusing times.

Chapter 2 identified new challenges for this age-old practice and asked the question, "Can managers be mentors?" It noted that in the twenty-first century the roles of manager, mentor, and leader are converging. Chapter 3 laid out the roles and responsibilities of mentors as change agents, as questioners, and as listeners, the very same critical roles that leaders are expected to assume in today's organizations.

This chapter identifies the values and skills of the mentor. It identifies the ideal character traits of the successful mentor and makes the link between manager, mentor, and leader at the level of competencies and skills.

As the world undergoes profound cultural changes wrought by globalization, new managers, who are a product of these changes, come equipped with a flexibility and adaptability to new workforce conditions that seasoned managers, steeped in the managerial virtues of planning, organizing, coordinating, and controlling, may lack.

On the other hand, seasoned managers have a wealth of experience, much of which has made them humble and put them on a path toward wisdom. The development of these values requires time.

Both new and seasoned managers who would be mentors must reflect on their values and on their accumulation of competencies and skills and must consider how they might nurture them for successful managing, mentoring, and leading.

Here we speak of values as habits that people develop over a lifetime. These habits develop through the modeling of attitudes, beliefs, and behavior of others and are reinforced through the actions that people take in practical, specific situations.

A person can identify his values by reflecting on his habitual behavior. For example, a person who wonders how courageous he is, or how much of a risk taker, may examine his past history of saying what is on his mind, of asking questions when he does not understand, or of sharing a conviction when he does not know the opinions of others. A person who wonders about how open he is may consider how he handles differences of opinion. Does he try to understand the opinion he does not hold? Is he willing to imagine more than one valid viewpoint on an issue? Can he remember the nuances of opinions that differ from his own?

Three skills—listening, questioning, and reflection—dominate in the hierarchy of skills required by the manager and mentor. They are the links to the values—those things that are useful, good, just, and wise— and the capacity for acting capably in a given situation. These skills allow the manager and mentor to assess how the employee/mentee manages with respect to his environment; help the mentor understand the mentee's relationships between his behavior, goals, and personal orientation; and facilitate the mentee's successful integration of skills, choices, and values.

Values flow through a mentor's skills. In reciprocal fashion, the practice of mentoring skills helps build and reinforce values in the manager and mentor.

Attributes/Values and Skills of the Mentor

Values

Service	Trust	Empowerment	
Humility	Openness	Curiosity	Courage
Integrity	Sensitivity	Balance	

Skills

Listening	Questioning	Goal setting
Managing differences	Building relationships	
Problem solving	Managing change	
Understanding/commitment to learning		
Facilitation	Analytical/systematic thinking	
Reflection/feedback	Advocacy	

VALUES

Just as the term *mentor* has its roots in Greek mythology, the values required of the manager as mentor transcend the workplace. They are habits that are celebrated and mythologized in every religion, every culture. These values—service, trust, empowerment, humility, openness, curiosity, courage, integrity, sensitivity, and balance in life—inform and inspire skills of the mentor. A brief examination of these values will set the stage for consideration of the skills the mentor uses in her relationship with her mentee.

Service

A good mentor both shares knowledge and wisdom and draws out the possibilities of those he/she mentors. There's an interest in and care for those he/she mentors as well as a willingness to hold down to the rigors of their discipline—there's that loving side and also that disciplining side.

—Laura Walters Baskett, associate chaplain and
director of church relations, University of Tulsa

Recent reports of highly visible executives who act as though a company belongs to them are superseded by executives who see themselves as servants to a corporate vision or a public good. Many executives strive to identify opportunities to promote the development of the employees who staff their organizations. Autry describes the servant leader, the one who empowers others, is concerned for their welfare, and is concerned that they have the tools and conditions to achieve their goals.[1]

The manager who models service is not one who has no other thought than to serve his colleagues. Rather this is a leader who has a broad vision for the company, who provides the encouragement, support, and power for others to achieve that vision. He is discerning, knowing what importance to give things; he gets outside of his own point of view and into the point of view of another. His judgment is free from ideology and personal agenda, and he is trusted by those he leads.

Trust

Few things help an individual more than to place responsibility upon him, and to let him know that you trust him.

—Booker T. Washington

The effective manager trusts her employees and they trust her. She keeps her word, and she keeps their confidence. She expects greatness of her employees. She has experienced the power and productivity of teams and knows she can delegate problems to her employees working in teams without doubt that they will find the best solutions.

In the trustful partnership between managers and employees and between mentors and mentees, error is accepted as a necessary part of the learning process. Neither party is afraid to take a risk because both understand that at the core of the relationship is a commitment to their common humanity.

As the manager takes risks, his employees will dare to take risks. As he learns from his mistakes, so will they. As he empowers them to learn and to develop, their trust and their loyalty to him and to their common vision also grow.

The mentor must be capable of modeling trust, a conviction that the mentee is capable not of avoiding error but of responsible self-direction with respect to learning and career development.

Mentors also model trust by being consistent, keeping promises and deadlines. Clear articulation of mentor/mentee roles and goals in the negotiation phase of the partnership can help build trust and keep the relationship open.

Empowerment

The desire to "do it my way" is critical to a mentee's sense of self....Doing something the mentor's way may lessen the mentee's sense of ownership. It may also be a way for him to avoid thought or responsibility....An effective mentor lets go or, more importantly, does not take charge of the mentee.

—Gordon Shea, *Mentoring*, p. 22

Empowering managers disdain the image of the corporate ladder. They know that power is not something found at the end of a long upward climb by means of a path that only one person may pass at a time. They also know that power is not a limited commodity, that it can be created, and that sharing power increases their power.

In an environment where power is unlimited, people who work together for mutual benefit empower one another. The manager who delegates, provides learning opportunities, and celebrates the achievements and accomplishments of others is endowed by them with even more power. The influence of the empowering manager over her employees far surpasses the authority endowed by her position.

Partnership-driven mentors empower and expect mentees to take control over their learning processes. They empower mentees by giving them encouragement, support, and honest feedback—those dynamics that are at the heart of the mentoring relationship.

In a society that features low self-esteem among two-thirds of its population, empowering mentors can bolster self-confidence among mentees by:

- refraining from judgment when the mentee vents negative feelings or presents partially reasoned conclusions,
- providing ideas for solving problems when asked, and
- offering help (as the mentee needs it) once the person has decided on a problem-solving course of action.[2]

Humility

It is unwise to be too sure of one's own wisdom. It is healthy to be reminded that the strongest might weaken and the wisest might err.

—Mohandas K. Gandhi

Humility is not timidity or meekness but is the antipathy of arrogance. Humility strengthens the mentoring relationship as the mentor eschews self-importance and models a hunger for knowledge and openness to the mentee's attitudes and ideas.

Sir Isaac Newton gave credit for his scientific success to his historical mentors in saying, "If I have seen farther (than you and Descartes) it is by standing upon the shoulders of Giants."

Humility may even involve sacrifice of personal comfort and perquisites of rank in order to meet the stewardship responsibilities inherent to positions of command and leadership.[3]

Mentors take learning seriously, but they do not take themselves seriously. They are as amused with their mistakes as with those of their mentees. Admission of mistakes can reduce mentees' tension and open channels to risk taking and learning.

Humility enables the mentor to model authenticity and realness. Alert to, yet comfortable with, his limitations, the mentor has no need to set himself up as the standard to which the mentee aspires. If mentors find themselves saying "You should..." or "I want you to...," they may lack humility. Humility frees the mentor for risk taking, prevents him from being the expert, and shatters power and distance barriers between him and the mentee. Humility also prevents the mentor from becoming an imposter, the one who would be all things to his mentee.[4]

Openness

Successful mentors recognize, understand, and model the qualities of a mentor-mentee relationship based on discovery and learner independence. They are open to alternative views and unique interpretations. Openness refers also to sharing information and feelings so that mentees are not confused about the message the mentor intends.

Mentors who recognize that both they and their mentees are in a lifelong process of learning and self-development are likely to remain open and to model openness in the mentoring relationship.

An open mentoring relationship inspires trust in both partners as they share ideas, suggestions, concerns, fears, and joys freely, confident that the other will neither pass judgment on these expressions nor violate the other's confidence.

Curiosity

It is a miracle that curiosity survives formal education.

—Albert Einstein

Many mentees come to the mentoring partnership without a well-developed sense of curiosity. Over the course of many years, parents and authority figures at school or church may have given the message that too many questions, or difficult questions, are not welcome. Mentees may have lost the passion to question, explore, and discover.

Mentors can model curiosity—that questioning openness to the world, to possibilities, and to surprises. The curiosity of the mentor to examine and discover anew each idea, event, and possibility will embolden the mentee to discard the formal and structural impediments to curiosity that characterized much of his formal education and training.

Courage

Life shrinks or expands in proportion to one's courage.

—Anaïs Nin

Mentoring and learning take courage. Great mentors exhibit courage; they take risks with learning, showing boldness in their efforts, and they elicit courage in their mentees by the examples they set. Risk, the willingness to step forward without assurance of success, precedes learning, and the preamble to risk is courage.

Mentoring relationships call out the best in our abilities, attitudes, and aspirations. In a learning partnership, the mentor continually communicates that she believes in the mentee as learner. Successful mentoring partnerships rely on the courage of both partners to be open to new learning.

Kofman and Senge have noted that fear of risk taking can obstruct learning. "When we see that to learn, we must be willing to look foolish, to let another teach us, learning doesn't always look so good anymore.... [O]nly with the support and fellowship of another can we face the dangers of learning meaningful things."[5]

When mentors pose difficult questions, admit to ignorance, subject their own ideas to critical review, and invite mentees to join in the critique, they teach valuable lessons. They model the behavior that leads to learning and give permission for mentees to do the same. Such behavior encourages mentees to experiment with new perspectives and to move ahead.

Integrity

Neither prejudice nor bias (gender, racial, ethnic) can coexist with a mentoring partnership. Any mentor that cannot get past bias does himself and his mentee a service by terminating the relationship. Integrity also precludes procrastination and neglect. If mentors find themselves missing or rescheduling mentoring meetings or putting off needed conversations with mentees, they need to reexamine their readiness for mentoring.

Integrity also requires that the communication between partners is honest and straightforward. When either partner gives feedback, there is no confusion as to intent or meaning. Successful learning for both relies on a partnership marked by genuineness and candor.

Sensitivity

Sensitivity allows the manager to transcend his own ego needs and become a resource to others. The sensitive manager captures not just the words but also the feelings of her employees. She becomes immersed in their context and "sees" things the way they see them. Listening intently, she sees the world through her employees' eyes and brings the relationships to a deeper level of communication. The sensitive manager is free from self-absorption and attends to more universal, collective, or global concerns.

The sensitive mentor is empathetic. Equipped with the understanding of how the four basic emotions (fear, anger, grief, joy), even when repressed, can surface in the workplace, the manager/mentor listens for emotions and explores their impact on employees' thinking and behavior. The mentor is on the lookout for disappointment, embarrassment, resistance, or satisfaction, which influence the judgment and action choices of the mentee.

Balance in Life

The pathway to mentoring success is found between extremes. The balanced mentor steers clear of extremes. He neither seeks to dominate his mentee nor to disengage from him. He seeks a relationship of mutuality, one that respects both parties and allows each to learn. A learning partnership is a balanced alliance, nurturing mutual interests, interdependence, and respect for differences.

Both managers and mentors veer to one extreme when they rely on their status or authority to impress or influence mentees. They visit the other extreme when they become indifferent to mentees, allowing them to wander without guidance or feedback. A balanced learning partnership features a spirit of generosity and energizes both partners.

Mentors respect mentees who exhibit extreme views, but their questioning seeks to help mentees move toward more balanced positions.

SKILLS

As mentors are guided by and, through practice, deepen their values of service, trust, empowerment, humility, openness, curiosity, courage, integrity, sensitivity, and balance in life, they become more competent in the skills that make them effective mentors, managers, and leaders: listening, questioning, setting goals and expectations, managing differences, building relationships and environment, problem solving, managing change, understanding and commitment to learning, facilitation, analytical and systemic thinking, reflection and feedback, and advocacy. Their improvement in these skill areas, in turn, sharpens and deepens the values they model to their colleagues, employees, and mentees.

Managers mentor formally and informally by exercising skills they have developed through their personal and professional experience. Here we examine briefly those skills that characterize the effective mentor and note that they enhance the superior functioning of managers as well.

Listening

The capacity to listen is at the heart of the mentoring relationship. When mentees believe that mentors are listening, they are likely to disclose all sorts of details about themselves and their ambitions. At this stage the real mentoring process can begin.

The mentor, listening respectfully, becomes absorbed in what the mentee says and comes to see the issue as the mentee sees it. Mentors listen for content, for context, and for tone.

Context. Here the mentor asks herself:

1. Why is my mentee telling me this?
    - Is he trying to impress me? Persuade me?
    - Is he seeking my approval?
2. Are these the mentee's convictions or someone else's?
3. How does the mentee structure and organize his information?

Content. With respect to content, the mentor wonders:

1. What is the mentee really saying?
2. What is the basis and flow of his argument or reasoning?
3. How much is unsubstantiated opinion? How much is factual?
4. On what assumptions is the mentee basing his argument?
5. Is all the information relevant?

Tone. Here the mentor asks himself:

1. Is the mentee's tone of voice appropriate to his statements?
2. What feelings are attendant to his statements?
3. Does the mentee use words with more than one meaning?

The most basic and powerful way to connect to another person is to listen. Just listen. Perhaps the most important thing we ever give each other is our attention.... A loving silence often has far more power to heal and to connect than the most well-intentioned words.

—Rachel Naomi Remen

The best managers and mentors are not necessarily the smartest or the most technically skilled people on the job. Management and mentoring are relational processes more than technical ones. Managers and mentors can, over time, learn to listen well. Seldin provides suggestions for managers and mentors to improve their listening skills.

1. Commit yourself to becoming a better listener. This means really listening and understanding, not just acting as if you are listening.
2. Let your mentee know of your intent to listen carefully to him.
3. Create the time, space, and privacy within which to listen.
4. Eliminate environmental distractions and interruptions. Disarming the cell phone is a powerful statement in this busy world of ours.
5. Open your mind and set aside assumptions and early analysis.
6. Listen for the whole message.
7. Do listening checks, as appropriate. "Let me be sure I understand. Do you mean _____?"
8. Ask for feedback. "Did I understand what you said?"[6]

Effective listening requires:

Concentration: A focus on the speaker by eliminating or ignoring internal distractions (one's own thoughts) and environmental disruptions.

Acknowledgment: A verbal and nonverbal demonstration of the mentor's active interest and attention.

Research: The mentor gathers information about her mentee through skillful questioning.

Emotional control: The mentor, like everyone else, reacts to emotionally charged words, phrases, and gestures. She may also react to body type, posture, and poor grammar. The mentor must control these reactions as part of effective listening.

Sensing: The mentor "listens" carefully to body language (those nonverbal messages) as well as to speed, volume, pitch, rhythm, inflection, and clarity. These identify the mentee's emotional state and intent.

Structure: The mentor also pays attention to the structure of the mentee's messages to learn how the mentee reasons, how he progresses from point to point, and his ability to distill and integrate ideas.

Mentors should take notes without distracting the mentee. The notes should be concise and focus only on the main points. The necessary details should be included within this framework. The act of preparing notes will help improve the quality of listening itself.

The mentor must also listen to himself to be able to understand and moderate, if necessary, the impact he has on the mentee. Through reflection on his interaction with the mentee, he assesses his practical abilities to suspend judgment, acknowledge emotion, be empathetic, "hear" between the lines, and provide appropriate feedback.

The mentor is not a therapist and should not play the role of a therapist. His sensitivity to the mentee's feelings is part of his effort to develop an integral understanding of the mentee's needs, capabilities, and progress in meeting his learning goals.

Mentors may listen differently to short- and long-term mentees. For example, in mentoring relationships of a year or more, the mentor will listen for gradual changes in the mentee and will improve his ability to pick up the mentee's verbal and nonverbal signals. This will enhance the mentor's ability to assist the learning goals of the mentee.

Questioning

One who asks a question is a fool for five minutes; one who does not ask a question remains a fool forever.

—Chinese proverb

Chapter 3 noted the powerful effect of questions in the learning process. A mentor's questions—especially open-ended, penetrating, and challenging questions—honor, respect, and empower the mentee. Questioning aids the mentor to avoid solving the mentee's problems, keeps him from passing judgment on the mentee's conclusions, and confirms his conviction that the mentee can identify internal and external resources to bring to bear on his learning needs.

Mentors ask questions that are obvious and not so obvious, they ask questions that encourage consideration of alternatives, and they ask questions that push the mentee to think systematically and to explore options before taking action.

Questions encourage the mentee to expand both time and space as environments in which to examine and resolve his problems.

Accomplished mentors find that they can facilitate the mentoring relationship, provide feedback, stimulate reflection, assist with goal setting and problem solving, evaluate, challenge, and guide mentees largely through the questioning process.

Setting Goals and Expectations

Much of the goal setting with respect to the mentoring relationship takes place in the negotiating phase. This provides an opportunity for the mentor to model realism, critical thinking, and a sense of perspective. Just as the goals of the relationship need to be clear and achievable so should be the learning goals the mentee sets for himself.

Here, too, the mentor must guard against doing too much for the mentee. Mentors may not want to shield mentees from the same mistakes they made earlier in their careers. They may want to protect the mentee from discouragement or disappointment. Usually, with questions and reflection, the mentor can help the mentee set goals that are appropriate, realistic, and achievable.

Managing Differences

Differences in the mentoring relationship may arise from a number of sources. Seeds of conflict may be embedded in the diverse personalities of mentor and mentee and play out in communication tone or style or in attitudes toward work, the organization, or the terms of the relationship. Partners may have differing or changing understandings of the roles and goals originally negotiated. Conflict may also arise from issues external to the relationship. The personal lives of either party may create stress that has an impact on the relationship.

Mentors should not shy away from addressing differences. Managing differences involves managing different viewpoints and recognizing that understanding different points of view, not eliminating them, is part of the mentoring partnership.

As the workplace becomes more diverse, managers and mentors must come to appreciate viewpoints or orientations that may be gender, race, or culture based. Mentors and managers must be aware of their own assumptions and biases so as not to inject these into relationships with employees and mentees.

Building Relationships and Environment

Successful managers and mentors are cognizant of the impact of organizational culture on learning in the workplace. If:

- the organization is hierarchical in its power structure,
- top executives are inaccessible to employees,
- communication between departments is closed or limited,
- there is no sustained institutional commitment to learning or development, and
- there is little awareness of the impact of globalization on the organization,

then the task of the manager to foster a learning environment will be an uphill struggle.

What can managers do in such an environment? Starting within their own realm of authority, there are a number of counterculture measures they can take. They can empower their own staff in small ways by:

- creating teams and providing opportunities for staff to function as team leaders;
- opening up the agenda at staff meetings;
- delegating responsibilities for planning, problem solving, and iden- tification of learning opportunities;
- using action learning to address problems; and
- building coalitions with fellow managers.

When the manager turns the office into a mini learning organization, he gives employees important messages:

- Empowerment need not be a top-down dynamic.
- Employees can be empowered to change organizational culture.
- The cultural environment of the organization has a major impact on employee learning, functioning, and attitudes toward work and self- confidence.

Mentors establish similar environments for mentees when they:

- encourage self-directed learning approaches;
- respect mentee's control of goal setting and action; and
- provide insightful, but not judgmental, feedback.

A major consulting firm found that professional reading among em- ployees increased when the firm installed magazine racks with profes- sional journals in the lavatories.... Employees began contributing their own copies of journals to which the firm did not subscribe. Comments like "Did you read that article about...?" were frequently interjected in staff meetings, which further reinforced the amount of informal learning through journal reading.

Managers and mentors create environments wherein employees can learn and grow by building positive relationships and fostering alliances and partnerships with colleagues at all organizational levels to create learning opportunities. These partnerships are grounded in mutual inter- ests, interdependence, and respect.

Problem Solving

Most of the advice given to mentors with respect to problem solving is contained in a pithy statement: "Don't do it!" Mentors should not solve problems for mentees because doing so can undermine the development of mentees' self-direction, confidence, and learning.

Nevertheless, the mentor should nourish her own problem-solving skills because she can then better assist her mentee to develop his. Well-developed problem-solving skills will assist the mentor to:

- provide appropriate information,
- encourage exploration of options, and
- ask penetrating questions. Questions that help mentees solve problems may include:

  1. Have you ever faced a problem such as this?
  2. What strategies have you used in the past to address a problem such as this?
  3. What resources are at your disposal to address this problem?
  4. What kind of result are you looking for?

If the mentor perceives that the mentee is making poor choices in problem solving, she may continue with questioning to help the mentee broaden his viewpoint or range of options. She may ask, "In choosing this course of action, what is the potential impact on yourself, on your colleagues, on other potential options?"

Mentors should retain confidence that mentees can and will make sound decisions, given appropriate exploration of context, information, and options. The mentor's intervention should focus not on giving advice or influencing the mentee's choices but on how to identify and assess options.

Mentors may encounter mentees whose self-confidence is so low that they have adopted patterns of self-defeating behavior and have trouble identifying viable courses of action. In these cases, it is tempting to tell the mentee what to do. The mentor may need to remind himself that failure is not the worst thing that can happen. The mentor can relate past failures of his own, and they can reflect on the mentee's past failures together, identifying negative behaviors and exploring alternative behaviors. Though he may feel compelled to rescue the mentee from failure, doing so will not contribute to the mentee's developing habits of positive problem solving and effective behavior.[7]

Managing Change

Change is a constant in today's organizations, and managers who once directed resources and organizational processes now must maintain vision and identify order in seemingly chaotic environments, and they must comanage change with their colleagues. The mentoring relationship plays out in this environment of change. Thus the mentoring partners must:

1. identify, as they can, changes affecting the workplace;
2. understand the impact of these changes on mentees and their career options; and
3. identify strategies and coping mechanisms to help mentees negotiate and manage change.

In the Industrial Age, a manager's ability to create a stable environment through judicious direction and control of the production process helped foster a compliant and calm demeanor among employees. In the knowledge age, a rapid-change environment may require that mentors help mentees expand their range of positive coping mechanisms and avoid counterproductive ones.[8]

Understanding and Commitment to Learning

Mentors and managers who facilitate learning provide a crucial service in this era of rapid change and increasing organizational complexity. Employees who do not grow will be unable to cope, adapt, and succeed. Mentors and managers should be alert for opportunities for discovery; learning opportunities abound in the actions that are part of employees' and mentees' daily work lives. Their actions and the choices that engendered them (as well as the ones left behind) are valuable objects of reflection.

Managers and mentors should also be vigilant for signs that learning is not taking place: apathy, cynicism, dullness. Consequently, they should be prepared to reignite the passion for learning or address the negative effects of an organizational culture that does not encourage the acquisition of new learning.

The mentor understands from her own experience that learning culminates in and is sustained by action. Thus the goal of mentoring is the development of the learner into a high-performing and highly productive and effective employee. Effective mentors look to the workplace itself as a stimulus to learning. A mentor may give an assignment or encourage the mentee to design a project. As this project or assignment unfolds, the mentor helps the mentee reflect on what he is doing effectively, what he is learning, and how he might improve his performance.

Finally, the mentor is committed to his own learning and sees opportunities to learn from the mentee and by reflecting on the quality of the relationship between them. As he expands and deepens his learning about effective mentoring, he becomes more effective as a manager.

Facilitation

Facilitation signifies the process by which mentors enable learning, and it is the heart of the enabling phase of mentoring. In concept a simple notion, "making it easy" for the mentee to learn, in action it is rife with complexity and nuance. Facilitation draws on all the mentor's skills and requires vigilance and restraint.

The vigilant mentor anticipates obstacles that might prevent the mentee from reaching her learning goals. Obstacles may be a part of the organizational culture or may be embedded in the mentee's attitudes and beliefs. The mentor must be prepared to help identify organizational obstacles and to challenge those erected by the mentee himself.

Mentors should exercise vigilance lest mentees draw inappropriate learning conclusions or stray from their original goals. With skillful questioning and reflection mentors can usually head off mentees' long journeys on roads that go nowhere.

Bell notes that mentors must also be vigilant for the teachable moment—that time when the mentee is ready to learn—or those conditions that are likely to support learning. He cautions mentors to:

- Stay vigilant for every opportunity to derive new learning.
- Keep a lookout for signs that a mentee has reached a plateau or barrier to learning. These may include apathy, boredom, or dullness.
- Listen carefully for answers to questions you did not ask. A question about work challenges, for example, may reveal a mentee's preoccupation with lack of confidence.
- Watch the mentee at work. The most effective interventions can result from observing mentee behavior in the workplace.[9]

Self-directed learning is a challenge for all learning facilitators, including mentors. They must provide encouragement, know when to question and challenge, and know when to seek feedback, lest they become obstacles to learning.

The mentor makes it easier for the mentee to learn, but learning is not always pain free. Frequently, significant growth occurs as the mentee struggles for understanding or deals with his roadblocks to learning. Mentors can relate instances of painful discoveries in their own lives to make it easier for mentees to face the risk taking in learning.

Of course, the goal of mentoring is not simply learning. It is also the development of the learner into a high-performing, more productive, and effective employee. Effective mentors look to the workplace itself as a stimulus to learning for mentees. A mentor may give an assignment or encourage the mentee to design a project. As the project or assignment unfolds, the mentor helps the mentee reflect on what he is doing effectively, what he is learning, and how he might improve his performance. These are the orientation and skills the mentee carries forward after the partnership has concluded.

Analytical and Systemic Thinking

Often, solutions to problems emerge when the context in which the problem is presented becomes clear. Leaders, managers, and mentors should be able to see the environment, the context in which organizational issues and events play out and in which employees learn and develop. Sometimes referred to as "seeing the big picture," and sometimes a catchword for logical thinking, systemic thinking comprises both of these.

The systemic thinker is action oriented but does not rush to judgment. She considers a problem from various viewpoints, relates it to other problems and their resolutions, frees her mind for fresh perspectives, and even wonders "what would Grandma think of this?" She also checks for inferences, truth, and validity of argument in proposed solutions to problems.

Mentors assist mentees to adopt systemic thinking skills by:

- exploring options before acting;
- helping the mentee articulate his environment, recognizing that in the age of knowledge organizational context can shift with stunning rapidity; and
- responding appropriately to the context in which the mentee functions.

Mentors can model the use of imagination and can reflect on their own experiences as a way of assisting mentees to function successfully in the midst of organizational change.

Reflection and Feedback

Reflection casts a new look at the content, context, and meaning of what has happened. It reinforces the intentional link between learning and action. It stimulates action and further learning.

Adults learn and retain knowledge best when they consciously reflect on their learning. Reflection stimulates questions, assesses learning, and enables the integration of new learning. Reflection in a mentoring relationship empowers both mentor and mentee.

For the mentor, reflection informs and strengthens the facilitation process. A reflective mentor finds herself more focused in her mentoring relationship. She is more energetic, takes more informed action, and will experience greater satisfaction with her mentoring relationship. Mentors who exercise and deepen their capacity for reflection will carry this competency into other personal and professional relationships.[10]

Mentors who reflect on their own experiences and learn from them will model critical reflection in the mentoring relationship. The reflective mentor both models reflection and facilitates its development by the mentee. The mentor should be comfortable asking questions such as:

- How are we doing as a partnership?
- How can we improve our performance?
- What has been the impact of this relationship on your learning goals?

These questions encourage the mentee to appreciate the power of reflection and integrate it into his learning process.

Mentors help mentees reflect by scheduling time for reflection, by keeping journals of their mentoring sessions, by coming to meetings prepared, and by beginning meetings with a progress review from the mentee and a relationship review from both.[11] Mentors who understand the confidence-building capacity of effective listening will not be overwhelmed by a mentee's discouragement or venting of negative feelings. They will not rush in with remedies to troublesome issues, but with careful listening, questioning, and reflection they will help the mentee devise her effective solutions for herself.

A major responsibility of the mentor is to provide feedback to the mentee. Giving specific, explicit, and timely feedback is a skill that some mentors find elusive. Furthermore, giving honest feedback can be uncomfortable for both mentors and mentees.

Feedback, offered graciously, is a gift that either partner can bestow on the other. Ongoing, honest, constructive feedback from both parties promotes competence, inspires confidence, and enriches the learning of both. Mentors should be prepared to model the giving of feedback and to give it such a way so as not to undermine the mentee's efforts to achieve his goals.

Feedback is distinguished from criticism, which is evaluative and judgmental. When a mentee is not performing well, the mentor should offer information, but not criticism. Providing feedback that is not criticism requires skill on the mentor's part.

When a mentor works hard to give feedback to a mentee in a way that is caringly frank and straightforward, or when a mentor implores her mentee for candid feedback, she is communicating clearly and plainly. The learning path is illuminated by the mentor's genuineness and candor.

Mentees may react strongly to feedback, especially if they perceive it as threatening. A mentee may not be able to accept feedback as accurate or relevant and may seem surprised by it. Mentors should be prepared to present specific information linked to mentees' statements and behavior that occasioned the feedback.

Feedback can free mentees from blocks by confirming self-assessments and can be excellent opportunities for mentors to open dialogue to new courses of action.

Action is the ultimate goal of feedback. The mentor encourages a mentee to move forward to meet new challenges and, as the feedback cycle begins again, asks reflective questions, helping the mentee integrate new learning. Feedback, given well, is really an opportunity for reflection in action.

"You had your evaluation today, Wendy?"

"We both focused on how we feel the relationship has gone, whether Karl's learning objectives have been achieved, what might have gone better, and how we both can apply the learning we gained to the workplace. Karl really is more confident and open, and he is much more devoted to the organization now because he sees how he can achieve his vision by staying with it."

"What did you learn about yourself," asked Wayne.

"My mentee admitted that I am a bit 'momish,' but he also said he really appreciated it, considering what he was going through in his personal life. It didn't seem like criticism. But I will work at being a bit less 'rescuing' and more empowering. I think that's one thing you have been good about, Wayne."

"Well, Jocelyn makes that easy because she is so self-directing in her learning. We are going to get together for lunch with several other mentor/mentee pairs to celebrate our accomplishments as part of closure."

Mentors must be prepared to take risks. Giving feedback concerning an assessment of a mentee's learning or behavior always carries risks. The mentor must have the courage to state her appraisal truthfully; a mentee who is not clear about the feedback will not benefit from it.

On occasion, feedback may involve confrontation. The mentor may feel compelled to challenge a mentee's attitude, behavior, or actions, especially if they seem counterproductive to the mentee's stated goals. The mentor may chose to cast the challenge in a series of questions that lead the mentee to examine the potential impact of his behavior or attitude on the outcomes he identified in the negotiation phase.

Finally, the mentor must enable the mentee to see feedback as a mutual activity. She may do this by making her questions inclusive. For example, the mentor may ask questions such as:

- How are we doing in this relationship?
- How can we improve the quality of the mentoring interaction?
- How can we improve the level of trust in this relationship?
- How has feedback been helpful so far?

Advocacy

Mentors are advocates for their mentees' learning and development. Advocacy may encompass confidence building, challenging, motivating, and inspiring. Advocacy may mean attendance at a mentee's marketing presentation or book signing. Although mentors may stop short of cheerleading, they let their mentees know how excited they are with their performance.

Advocacy may involve identifying and facilitating learning opportunities for mentees, arranging introduction to experts or other high performers in the mentee's field. Mentors may invite mentees, as observers or even as presenters, to organizational meetings or to symposia outside the organization.

Within the mentoring partnership the mentor is especially an advocate for learning. Mentors create an environment that values and nurtures learning. The mentor may encourage and challenge the mentee to pursue his ideas, may share books and articles, or may bring into the mentoring conversation news or current events that are related to the mentee's learning goals.

As advocates, mentors may also put mentees in touch with other organizational units that can enhance the mentee's experiential learning. Such activities can cement mentees' learning by encouraging them to act on what they have learned.

As advocates, mentors should be skilled networkers and have a sizable network of diverse contacts.

THE MENTOR'S IMPACT

There is a great person who makes everyone feel small. But the really great person is the one who makes everyone feel great.

—Chinese proverb

The mentor is on the path to wisdom, the culmination of her values and skills. She continually changes her life in small ways through the exercise of her skills, especially the deepening of her capacity to listen and to question.

The incremental changes in the life of the mentor increase her capacity to understand her mentee's needs, and challenge and empower the mentee to become more capable of identifying, refining, and directing his learning and career goals.

By recognizing and affirming the needs, fears, successes, and setbacks of the mentee who adapts to the changing environment of his personal and professional life, the mentor encourages the mentee to develop and grow in learning and understanding. By modeling skills, competencies, and virtues, the mentor invites the mentee to set even higher expectations of himself and his capacity to contribute and succeed.

Mentors should be good communicators, listen actively, possess the ability to relate to others, and be nonjudgmental. Mentors should have a genuine desire to be part of other peoples' lives, to help them pursue their interests, achieve their career goals, and handle tough decisions. A mentor should also be committed to his or her own development and have the time to invest to make a mentoring relationship work.

The virtues and skills required of the mentor can be modeled. Most of us know open, curious, empowering, or humble people, and we can challenge and encourage ourselves and others to develop these characteristics. We can become ever more discriminating in our ability to see the world on its own terms or as others see it (curiosity, sensitivity, humility) and can become ever more able to make sense of it despite its growing complexity—able to make sense of it in ways that both retain our own sense of meaning and yet respect its diversity (courage, openness, balance). We can make ourselves into successful mentors, as we shall see in the following chapters.

PART II

Action Plan, Tools, and Resources

In part I, we presented the key theories, principles, and practices of mentoring. In part II, you will have the opportunity to determine your readiness to be a mentor (chapter 5), develop action plans to enhance your skills as a mentor (chapter 6), and identify and utilize appropriate tools to enhance those skills (chapter 7). Finally, in chapter 8 we provide an array of informational resources of books and Web sites to further assist you in your journey to become a successful manager/mentor.

FIVE

Assessing Yourself as a Mentor

Potential mentors must ask themselves whether they are ready, willing, and able to mentor others. They must assess realistically whether they have the time, skills, and freedom to devote themselves to others. They must believe in the value of their work without worrying about returned favors. A manager who has a freely giving nature will probably mentor all through her life—probably without thinking much about it.

Great mentors know that they, as well as their mentees, are in a lifelong process of self-development. Managers who choose to take on the challenge of mentoring will have to sharpen their listening and coaching skills and learn or improve techniques of confrontation and resolving conflict. In effect, the mentees begin a journey of self-development.[1]

A great deal of the burden of success for a mentoring relationship falls upon the mentor who, as we have seen, must have or develop qualities of wisdom, courage, balance, humility, openness, and curiosity; must be competent in listening, questioning, and reflection; and must have or develop skill in brokering, facilitating, goal setting, managing conflict, problem solving, and advocacy.

So then, can only saints be mentors, or do all of us have the potential to be effective and successful mentors? Some people may have personalities or experiences that do not suit them to mentoring, but the majority of managers has likely developed many of these values and skills and with effort can improve their quality. As should be apparent, improving the values and skills that are needed for successful mentoring will also improve the values and skills of the effective manager.

This chapter provides some insight and advice on how to improve the skills needed for effective mentoring, suggests an action plan for improving mentoring ability, and refers to a number of assessment tools that can help the potential mentor better understand his strengths and development needs. As you may recall, in chapter 4 we identified a number of values and attributes that successful mentors exhibit. We also listed 12 specific skills necessary to successfully carry out the mentoring relationship. In this chapter, we have developed assessment instruments that will enable you to identify your strengths and areas for growth in each of the values and each of the skills.

ATTRIBUTES OF THE SUCCESSFUL MENTOR

Those who are successful mentors tend to possess and exhibit a number of attributes, virtues, and values that influence and guide their actions and the use of their skills. They become a part of their way of thinking and living; are developed through the modeling of attitudes, beliefs, and behavior of others; and are reinforced through the actions that people take in practical, specific situations.

As noted in Chapter 4, we have identified 10 attributes that should serve as the foundational values and core virtues for those managers who seek to become effective mentors:

1. Service mentality
2. Trust
3. Commitment to empowering others
4. Humility
5. Openness
6. Curiosity
7. Courage
8. Integrity
9. Sensitivity
10. Balance in life

Instructions: For the 10 attributes listed below, please read each statement and circle the number that best represents your behavior:

1—Never
2—Rarely
3—Sometimes
4—Most of the time
5—Always

1. Service Mentality	1 2 3 4 5
1. I am more focused on serving others than on meeting my own goals.	1 2 3 4 5
2. I promote others' success and am pleased when others are promoted to greater responsibility.	1 2 3 4 5
3. I strive to encourage and celebrate the accomplishments of others.	1 2 3 4 5

2. Trust	
4. I am comfortable in delegating important tasks to others.	1 2 3 4 5
5. I do not assume to know the intent of others' actions.	1 2 3 4 5
6. I have no need to micromanage.	1 2 3 4 5

3. Commitment to Empowering Others	
7. I allow, even encourage, my employees to take risks.	1 2 3 4 5
8. I strive not to stifle initiatives of employees.	1 2 3 4 5
9. I tell my employees that failures are opportunities to grow.	1 2 3 4 5

4. Humility	
10. I recognize that my success is built on the efforts of others.	1 2 3 4 5
11. I am comfortable in building on my mistakes.	1 2 3 4 5
12. I feel comfortable having my views challenged.	1 2 3 4 5

5. Openness	
13. I am open to other points of view.	1 2 3 4 5
14. I am comfortable admitting mistakes.	1 2 3 4 5
15. I learn and adopt opinions of my employees.	1 2 3 4 5

6. Curiosity	
16. I love to learn about new things.	1 2 3 4 5
17. I am comfortable in questioning assumptions, including my own.	1 2 3 4 5
18. I am interested in the motivation of others.	1 2 3 4 5

7. Courage

19. I am able to be wrong.	1 2 3 4 5
20. I respect others no matter what setting I am in.	1 2 3 4 5
21. I am willing to stand up for my colleagues.	1 2 3 4 5

8. Integrity

22. I keep my promises and do what I have said I will do.	1 2 3 4 5
23. I do not tell people what they want to hear.	1 2 3 4 5
24. What I expect from others is the same as what I expect from myself.	1 2 3 4 5

9. Sensitivity

25. I am able to see when people are hurt, affected, happy.	1 2 3 4 5
26. I recognize how feelings affect work.	1 2 3 4 5
27. I modify my style of communication to accommodate cultural diversity.	1 2 3 4 5

10. Balance in Life

28. I take time to read broadly, even outside my area of expertise.	1 2 3 4 5
29. I easily balance my family and work responsibilities.	1 2 3 4 5
30. I recognize the value of play, even at work.	1 2 3 4 5

Results

30–60	Mentoring is probably not for you.
61–90	You have some of the key values for becoming a mentor but will need to commit yourself and to take advantage of the tools and tips found in chapters 6 and 7.
91–120	You have potential to become an excellent manager/mentor.
121–150	You already possess the attributes to become a great mentor; you may need to work on the specific skills of the manager/mentor.

MENTORING SKILLS

Now that you have assessed yourself on the 10 attributes of the manager/mentor, let us examine the 12 skills that serve in enabling the manager/mentor to be effective in working with mentees.

1. Listening
2. Questioning
3. Setting goals and expectations

4. Managing differences
5. Building relationships and environment
6. Problem solving
7. Managing change
8. Understanding and commitment to learning
9. Facilitation
10. Analytical and systemic thinking
11. Reflection and feedback
12. Advocacy

1. Listening/Observing

Instructions: Please read each statement and circle the number that best represents your behavior:

1—Never
2—Rarely
3—Sometimes
4—Most of the time
5—Always

1. I recognize the importance of carefully listening to others.	1 2 3 4 5
2. I listen attentively so as to capture both verbal and nonverbal cues.	1 2 3 4 5
3. I summarize and articulate what I have heard.	1 2 3 4 5
4. I listen for content.	1 2 3 4 5
5. I listen for context.	1 2 3 4 5
6. I listen for tone.	1 2 3 4 5
7. I avoid doing other tasks so I can devote full visual attention to the person.	1 2 3 4 5
8. I am open to the ideas of others, even if they differ from my own.	1 2 3 4 5
9. I am willing to suspend judgment on what others say.	1 2 3 4 5
10. I do not interrupt but allow the other person to complete his thoughts.	1 2 3 4 5
11. I am patient.	1 2 3 4 5
12. I reinforce and validate the feelings and thoughts of others.	1 2 3 4 5
13. I avoid making conclusions and assumptions.	1 2 3 4 5
14. I seek input and inquire rather than advocate and instruct.	1 2 3 4 5
15. I demonstrate listening by asking questions about what has been said.	1 2 3 4 5

Scoring Results

Under 30	You have difficulty in listening to others.
30–45	You have some skills in listening.
46–60	You are a good listener.
61–75	You are a great listener.

2. Questioning

Instructions: Please read each statement and circle the number that best represents your behavior:

1—Never
2—Rarely
3—Sometimes
4—Most of the time
5—Always

1. I recognize the importance and impact of asking questions.	1 2 3 4 5
2. I am comfortable in asking questions.	1 2 3 4 5
3. I am comfortable in being asked questions.	1 2 3 4 5
4. I try to avoid asking evaluative or closed-minded questions.	1 2 3 4 5
5. I ask questions to discover new information and the truth rather than just to confirm my conclusions and biases.	1 2 3 4 5
6. I like to ask questions that enable my subordinates/ colleagues to work together.	1 2 3 4 5
7. I listen carefully to responses to my questions.	1 2 3 4 5
8. I ask empowering questions.	1 2 3 4 5
9. I encourage questions from others.	1 2 3 4 5
10. I am patient when awaiting responses to my questions.	1 2 3 4 5
11. I have the courage to ask challenging, fresh questions.	1 2 3 4 5
12. I ask questions that help to clarify and summarize.	1 2 3 4 5
13. My questions are clear and open.	1 2 3 4 5
14. The timing of my questions is appropriate.	1 2 3 4 5
15. I ask investigative and discovery questions.	1 2 3 4 5

Scoring Results

Under 30	You have much to learn about questioning.
30–45	You have some understanding of and skills in questioning.
46–60	You have the potential to be an effective questioner.
61–75	You are already a good questioner.

3. Setting Goals and Expectations

Instructions: Please read each statement and circle the number that best represents your behavior:

1—Never
2—Rarely
3—Sometimes
4—Most of the time
5—Always

1. I recognize the importance of setting goals.	1 2 3 4 5
2. I set goals that are measurable.	1 2 3 4 5
3. I set goals that are achievable.	1 2 3 4 5
4. I set goals that are realistic and flexible.	1 2 3 4 5
5. I set goals that have clear time frames.	1 2 3 4 5
6. I set goals that are connected to performance.	1 2 3 4 5
7. I set goals that are challenging.	1 2 3 4 5
8. I mutually set goals that have the support and concurrence of the other person.	1 2 3 4 5
9. I set expectations that include learning from experiences, both successes and failures.	1 2 3 4 5
10. I review, modify, and update goals.	1 2 3 4 5
11. I put goals into writing so all parties are clearly aware of them.	1 2 3 4 5
12. I reinforce the achievement of goals through recognition, rewards, and other internal and external motivators.	1 2 3 4 5
13. I identify the in-house and external resources needed to achieve the goals.	1 2 3 4 5
14. I help to identify obstacles to achieving the goals.	1 2 3 4 5
15. I assist in identifying resources in achieving the goals.	1 2 3 4 5

Scoring Results

Under 30	You have little understanding of goal setting.
30–45	You understand the basics of goal setting.
46–60	You have good skills.
61–75	You already have strong goal-setting skills.

4. Managing Differences

Instructions: Please read each statement and circle the number that best represents your behavior:
1—Never
2—Rarely
3—Sometimes
4—Most of the time
5—Always

1. I recognize and welcome different attitudes, styles, and values in the workplace.	1 2 3 4 5
2. I am a skilled negotiator.	1 2 3 4 5
3. I help my colleagues/staff clarify their attitudes, thinking, and values.	1 2 3 4 5
4. I am sensitive to the need to identify and/or seek common ground in a diverse setting.	1 2 3 4 5
5. I am able to foster dialogue rather than debate (tool: dialogue vs. debate).	1 2 3 4 5
6. I state my needs without arguing.	1 2 3 4 5
7. I can see myself as others see me.	1 2 3 4 5
8. I can recognize and change in myself that which I do not like.	1 2 3 4 5
9. I am comfortable with compromise.	1 2 3 4 5
10. My self-confidence is not threatened when others disagree with my position.	1 2 3 4 5
11. I recognize that a problem may have many successful solutions.	1 2 3 4 5
12. I can disagree with a colleague's position and still like or trust him/her.	1 2 3 4 5
13. I know what makes me angry or upset (hot-button exercise).	1 2 3 4 5
14. I have developed my understanding and skills in conflict management.	1 2 3 4 5
15. In a diverse work setting, I do not see everyone as the same.	1 2 3 4 5
16. I can change my communication style to accommodate cultural differences.	1 2 3 4 5
17. I am aware of my common assumptions and biases.	1 2 3 4 5

Scoring Results

Under 30	You have much to learn about managing differences.
30–45	You have some skills in managing differences.
46–60	You have the potential to manage differences effectively.
61–85	You successfully manage differences.

5. Building Relationships and Mentoring Environment

Instructions: Please read each statement and circle the number that best represents your behavior:

1—Never
2—Rarely
3—Sometimes
4—Most of the time
5—Always

1. I recognize the importance of creating a supportive environment. 1 2 3 4 5

2. I make an effort to build a supportive relationship. 1 2 3 4 5

3. I prepare for the initial interaction. 1 2 3 4 5

4. I provide structure and assure timing, logistics, and work space for the meetings. 1 2 3 4 5

5. I seek to maintain positive relationships even when there are disagreements and differences. 1 2 3 4 5

6. I follow through on my commitments. 1 2 3 4 5

7. I have a service mentality and focus on the concerns of the other person. 1 2 3 4 5

8. I do not need to control the situation. 1 2 3 4 5

9. I do not seek to create dependency. 1 2 3 4 5

10. I have a healthy appreciation of different cultures and values. 1 2 3 4 5

11. I provide for a secure, confidential setting and atmosphere. 1 2 3 4 5

12. I check out how the other person feels about the environment and relationship. 1 2 3 4 5

13. I encourage and support change. 1 2 3 4 5

14. I provide support in difficult and painful situations. 1 2 3 4 5

Scoring Results

Under 30   You have little understanding of building relationships.
30–45   You understand the basics of building relationships.
46–60   You have good relationship-building skills.
61–70   You already have strong relationship-building skills.

6. Problem Solving

Instructions: Please read each statement and circle the number that best represents your behavior:

1—Never
2—Rarely
3—Sometimes
4—Most of the time
5—Always

1. I employ the holistic approach to problem solving.	1 2 3 4 5
2. I ask penetrating questions.	1 2 3 4 5
3. I explore a wide array of options.	1 2 3 4 5
4. I utilize a variety of problem-solving techniques.	1 2 3 4 5
5. I search for creative solutions.	1 2 3 4 5
6. I recognize the impact of actions and strategies on people and organizations.	1 2 3 4 5
7. I use systems thinking.	1 2 3 4 5
8. I gather data from a wide array of sources.	1 2 3 4 5
9. I am open to possible causes and solutions.	1 2 3 4 5
10. I allow affected persons to handle problems on their own.	1 2 3 4 5

Scoring Results

Under 20	You have difficulty in solving problems for yourself, much less in helping others.
20–30	You have grasped some of the essentials of problem solving.
31–40	You have some strong skills in problem solving.
41–50	You are already skilled in problem solving.

7. Managing Change

Instructions: Please read each statement and circle the number that best represents your behavior:

1—Never
2—Rarely
3—Sometimes
4—Most of the time
5—Always

1. I maintain a broad vision in a rapidly changing world.	1 2 3 4 5
2. I am adept at identifying changes in the workplace.	1 2 3 4 5
3. I am receptive and open to change.	1 2 3 4 5
4. I understand distrust and fear as reactions to change.	1 2 3 4 5
5. I work well with others to comanage change.	1 2 3 4 5
6. I appreciate the pressure that changes puts on employees and on organizational structures.	1 2 3 4 5
7. I am comfortable managing in an uncertain, chaotic environment.	1 2 3 4 5
8. I am comfortable with my core values in a changing workplace.	1 2 3 4 5
9. I am proactive, always searching for new ways to accomplish old tasks.	1 2 3 4 5
10. I help others to understand the impact of rapid change.	1 2 3 4 5
11. I am comfortable in spontaneous and ad hoc situations.	1 2 3 4 5
12. I welcome flextime, flex-place, and virtual offices.	1 2 3 4 5
13. I am comfortable in new and unfamiliar situations.	1 2 3 4 5
14. I can identify coping mechanisms and strategies in times of change.	1 2 3 4 5
15. I see change as a learning opportunity.	1 2 3 4 5

Scoring Results

Under 30	Little or no understanding or appreciation of change.
30–45	You are beginning to use change-management skills.
46–60	You have developed good change-management skills.
61–75	You already possess strong change-management skills.

8. Understanding and Commitment to Learning

Instructions: Please read each statement and circle the number that best represents your behavior:

1—Never
2—Rarely
3—Sometimes
4—Most of the time
5—Always

1. I recognize the importance of learning for short-term and long-term success.	1 2 3 4 5
2. I encourage reflection on successes and failures as an effective way to learn.	1 2 3 4 5
3. I connect learning to business goals and business goals to learning.	1 2 3 4 5
4. I see value in people discovering for themselves.	1 2 3 4 5
5. I see learning as a lifelong and continuous commitment.	1 2 3 4 5
6. I create an environment and continuous opportunities for learning.	1 2 3 4 5
7. I reward people for their learning.	1 2 3 4 5
8. I see learning as a joint responsibility and assist others in arranging for their learning.	1 2 3 4 5
9. I recognize that questions can enhance the learning of my colleagues.	1 2 3 4 5
10. I encourage the immediate application of learning.	1 2 3 4 5
11. I understand that deep and important learning involves the whole person—emotional, social, cognitive, and physical.	1 2 3 4 5
12. I see learning as open-ended.	1 2 3 4 5
13. I seek to create communities of practice.	1 2 3 4 5
14. I encourage people to share their learning.	1 2 3 4 5
15. I build action learning into day-to-day projects and crises.	1 2 3 4 5

Scoring Results

Under 30	Pedagogy, andragogy; all the same to you.
30–45	You understand some of the principles and practices of learning.
46–60	You have a good understanding of adult learning.
61–75	You are already practicing strong adult learning skills.

9. Facilitation

Instructions: Please read each statement and circle the number that best represents your behavior:
1—Never
2—Rarely
3—Sometimes
4—Most of the time
5—Always

1. I recognize the importance of setting schedules and retaining agreed-to meetings.	1 2 3 4 5
2. I manage time well to accomplish objectives.	1 2 3 4 5
3. I provide resources necessary for successful meetings.	1 2 3 4 5
4. I anticipate obstacles.	1 2 3 4 5
5. I determine the appropriate form/style of mentoring or counseling, be it structured or unstructured, short-term or long-term.	1 2 3 4 5
6. I can arrange and handle virtual meetings.	1 2 3 4 5
7. I can arrange and handle asynchronous meetings.	1 2 3 4 5
8. I work well with and enable others in handling logistics.	1 2 3 4 5
9. I plan and coordinate meetings with individuals and with groups in an efficient manner.	1 2 3 4 5
10. I facilitate discussion with questions.	1 2 3 4 5
11. I provide helpful and timely feedback during meetings.	1 2 3 4 5
12. Decisions made and responsibilities assigned are clear at meetings that I manage.	1 2 3 4 5
13. I am sensitive to the needs and interests of group members.	1 2 3 4 5
14. I communicate information in a timely manner.	1 2 3 4 5
15. I respond well to suggestions and criticisms.	1 2 3 4 5

Scoring Results

Under 30	Little or no understanding or appreciation of feedback.
30–45	You are beginning to use facilitation skills.
46–60	You have some good facilitation skills.
61–75	You are already a strong facilitator.

10. Analytical Thinking/Systems Thinking

Instructions: Please read each statement and circle the number that best represents your behavior:

1—Never
2—Rarely
3—Sometimes
4—Most of the time
5—Always

1. I am able to see the big picture as well as the micropicture.	1 2 3 4 5
2. I look for multiple causes.	1 2 3 4 5
3. I examine multiple impacts of actions taken.	1 2 3 4 5
4. I understand and utilize chaos theory and complexity theory.	1 2 3 4 5
5. I am able to isolate and integrate causes and effects.	1 2 3 4 5
6. I seek and can identify where greatest leverage can be applied.	1 2 3 4 5
7. I am able to see how to achieve the greatest benefits with least effort and least amount of time.	1 2 3 4 5
8. I am action oriented.	1 2 3 4 5
9. I consider problems from various viewpoints.	1 2 3 4 5
10. I am open to various strategies and solutions and perspectives.	1 2 3 4 5
11. I am creative.	1 2 3 4 5
12. I encourage creativity in others.	1 2 3 4 5
13. I appreciate the context of the environment and the culture.	1 2 3 4 5
14. I am comfortable in checking for truths other than my own.	1 2 3 4 5
15. I seek validity of arguments.	1 2 3 4 5

Scoring Results

Under 30	Little or no understanding or appreciation of feedback.
30–45	You are beginning to use facilitation skills.
46–60	You have some good facilitation skills.
61–75	You are already a strong facilitator.

11. Feedback and Reflection

Instructions: Please read each statement and circle the number that best represents your behavior:

1—Never
2—Rarely
3—Sometimes
4—Most of the time
5—Always

1. I encourage and foster reflection through insightful questions.	1 2 3 4 5
2. My feedback enables a person to be reflective and to learn.	1 2 3 4 5
3. I understand the importance of providing regular feedback.	1 2 3 4 5
4. I am aware of my feedback style.	1 2 3 4 5
5. I discuss the process and procedures for my providing of feedback.	1 2 3 4 5
6. I check out the timing and appropriateness of the feedback.	1 2 3 4 5
7. My feedback is honest, corrective, and authentic.	1 2 3 4 5
8. I provide feedback in an objective and nonjudgmental manner.	1 2 3 4 5
9. I link specific learning and action to the feedback.	1 2 3 4 5
10. My feedback is connected to the goals of my subordinate.	1 2 3 4 5
11. I focus my feedback on behavior and attitude, not on personality.	1 2 3 4 5
12. My feedback focuses on strengths as well as weaknesses.	1 2 3 4 5
13. I invite feedback on my feedback style.	1 2 3 4 5
14. I provide feedback as soon as possible.	1 2 3 4 5
15. I assist people to self-assess and provide feedback for themselves.	1 2 3 4 5

Scoring Results

Under 30	Little or no understanding or appreciation of feedback.
30–45	You are beginning to use facilitation skills.
46–60	You have some good facilitation skills.
61–75	You are already a strong facilitator.

12. Advocacy

Instructions: Please read each statement and circle the number that best represents your behavior:

1—Never
2—Rarely
3—Sometimes
4—Most of the time
5—Always

1. I motivate my employees and build their confidence.	1 2 3 4 5
2. I build and maintain diverse connections and networks.	1 2 3 4 5
3. I actively promote learning among my colleagues.	1 2 3 4 5
4. I introduce my employees to others who can help them.	1 2 3 4 5
5. I help others find learning resources.	1 2 3 4 5
6. I invite employees to meetings and events.	1 2 3 4 5
7. I clarify employees' needs/desires/goals.	1 2 3 4 5
8. With colleagues I model an appreciation of learning.	1 2 3 4 5
9. I encourage others to act on what they have learned.	1 2 3 4 5
10. I help others to believe in their potential and inspire them to reach it.	1 2 3 4 5
11. I attend employees' presentations and give them positive feedback.	1 2 3 4 5
12. I am my staff's biggest cheerleader.	1 2 3 4 5
13. I advocate for the promotion and development of my employees.	1 2 3 4 5
14. I work on building my network of contacts and resources.	1 2 3 4 5
15. I enjoy marketing talent around me.	1 2 3 4 5

Scoring Results

Under 30	Little or no understanding or appreciation of feedback.
30–45	You are beginning to use facilitation skills.
46–60	You have some good facilitation skills.
61–75	You are already a strong facilitator.

The above instrument provides you the opportunity to do an overall assessment of the 10 manager-mentee attributes. In the final column, begin identifying the specific knowledge or subskills that you now recognize are important to develop.

Assessing Your Overall Potential and Capabilities of Becoming an Effective Manager/Mentor

Mentoring Attributes Inventory and Planning Sheet

Values	Score	Specific Areas for Developing
Service		
Trust		
Empowerment		
Humility		
Openness		
Curiosity		
Courage		
Integrity		
Sensitivity		
Balance in life		

The final assessment instrument in this chapter is the Mentoring Skills Inventory and Planning Sheet. This instrument will be invaluable as you develop your action plans and choose strategies in chapter 6.

Mentoring Skills Inventory and Planning Sheet

Skill	Score	Specific Areas for Developing
Listening		
Questioning		
Setting goals and expectations		
Managing differences		
Building relationships and the mentoring environment		
Problem solving		
Managing change		
Understanding of and commitment to learning		
Facilitation		
Analytical and systems thinking		
Reflection and feedback		
Advocacy		

ANALYZING THE RESULTS

Based upon the results of the assessments included in this chapter, you are now able to determine your present capabilities in becoming a successful and effective mentor.

What Are Your Strengths and Areas for Improvement?

As you review your scores for each of the 10 values and 12 skills, look for those areas in which you are already quite competent. An important adage of self-development is to build on one's strengths as well as areas needing improvement. What are your strongest skills as well as the attributes in which you are already quite proficient? Next, examine which would be the attributes that you would be most eager to develop. We would suggest that you focus on five attributes and five skills.

Top Five Values/Attributes that I Seek to Develop/Improve

1.

2.

3.

4.

5.

Top Five Skills that I Seek to Develop/Improve

1.

2.

3.

4.

5.

NEXT STEPS

In chapter 6, you will have the opportunity to develop strategies and action plans for those attributes and skills that you have chosen. Chapter 7 provides an extensive set of tools, exercises, and information to assist in your action plan, and chapter 8 contains a list of books, Web sites, and other resources that will be invaluable for your further development as a manager who can effectively lead and serve as a mentor.

SIX

Developing an Action Plan and Identifying Strategies for Becoming an Effective Mentor

In chapter 5, you had the opportunity to assess yourself in each of the 12 skills of being a mentor as well as the 10 attributes necessary for being an effective manager/mentor. In this chapter, we provide the opportunity for you to identify resources and to develop action plans that will enable you to become an effective mentor.

WHAT IS AN ACTION PLAN?

An action plan is a way to make sure your goals are made concrete. It describes the way you will use strategies to meet your objectives. Each action step or change to be sought should include the following information:

- *What* actions or strategies will occur?
- *Who* will carry out these changes?
- *By when* will they take place and for how long?
- *What resources* (i.e., money, staff) are needed to carry out these changes?
- *Communication* (who should know what?).

Why should you develop an action plan? An inspirational adage states, "People don't plan to fail. Instead they fail to plan." Because you certainly do not want to fail, it makes sense to take all of the steps necessary to ensure success, including developing an action plan. Action plans help to make sure you do not overlook any of the details and to understand what is and what is not possible for you to do. Action plans allows you to be more efficient, to save time, energy, and resources in the long run. It also gives you some clarity and accountability to yourself.

It is important to remember, though, that an action plan is always a work in progress. It is not something you can write, lock in your file drawers, and forget about. Keep it visible. Display it prominently. As your mentoring experience and capability grow, you will want to continually (usually monthly) revise your action plan to fit your changing responsibilities.

STEPS FOR A MENTORING ACTION PLAN

The first step in developing yourself as a mentor is to assess your current level of capability relative to your mentoring values and your mentoring skills. Chapter 5 contained a number of instruments to allow you to do this. As you assess your mentoring capabilities, it is important to focus on your strengths as well as your weaknesses.

In developing an action plan, be sure to include action steps that address all capabilities you wish to improve. The plan should be complete, clear, and current. Here are some guidelines to follow to write action steps.

Be sure to keep track of what (and how well) you have done. Keep several questions in mind:

- Am I doing what I said I'd do?
- Am I doing it well?

Celebrate a job well done. Celebrate your accomplishments; you and those you work with deserve it. Celebration helps keep everyone excited and interested in the work they are doing.

In the pages that follow, we provide the reader with the opportunity to develop strategies and an action plan to improve your 10 attributes as well as each of the 12 skills necessary to become an effective manager/mentor.

In each instrument, you will note three columns. Column 1 (Areas for Improvement) contains a list of the attributes or the subskills and knowledge areas that form the substance of that particular skill. Circle those that you determine, based upon the assessment instruments of chapter 5, are most important to improve.

Column 2 (Resources and Strategies) provides a list of resources and tools that are found in chapter 7 and Web sites and books located in chapter 8. Greater details about the Web sites and books are included in chapter 8. Any and all of these resources and strategies can assist you in improving your capabilities in the respective skill areas.

Column 3 (Action Plan) contains a list of questions to guide you in the development of an action plan to develop that particular attribute and skill.

Mentoring Attributes

Areas for Improvement (circle those you would like to develop)	Resources and Strategies	Action Plan
• Service • Trust • Empowerment • Humility • Openness • Curiosity • Courage • Integrity • Sensitivity • Balance in life	Chapter 7 resources • *Mentoring Capabilities, Interests, and Resources* Web sites • http://www.mentoring group.com/home.html • http://www.mentoring.org • http://www.peer.ca/mentorpapers • http://www.mentors.net/03joinform.html • http://www.coaching network.org.uk/Default.htm Books • *The Mentor's Guide: Facilitating Effective Learning Relationships* • *Mentoring: How to Develop Successful Mentor Behaviors* • *Managers as Mentors: Building Partnerships for Learning* • *A Mentor's Companion*	• When? Time frame? • With whom? • How? • Resources needed? • How communicated? • How to determine if at desired level?

Mentoring Skills

In the following pages, we have provided a framework to assist you in developing an action plan to enhance each of the 12 mentoring skills.

Listening

Areas for Improvement (circle those you would like to develop)	Resources and Strategies	Action Plan
• Listening for tone • Listening for content • Listening for context • Listening for non-verbal language • Cultural listening and sensitivity • Paraphrasing and connecting	Chapter 7 resources • *Exercises for Essential Listening Skills* • *Active Listening Skills* • *Action Learning* Web site • http://www.businesslistening.com/ Book • *Listening Leaders: The Ten Golden Rules to Listen, Lead & Succeed*	• When? Time frame? • With whom? • How? • Resources needed? • How communicated? • How to determine if at desired level?

Questioning

Areas for Improvement (circle those you would like to develop)	Resources and Strategies	Action Plan
• Knowledge of types of questions • Creating comfort in receiving questions • Listening to questions • Building on questions • When to ask questions • How to ask questions	Chapter 7 resources • *Questions for the Mentee* • *Action Learning* • *Judging versus Learning Mindset for Asking Questions* Web site • http://www.inquiryinc.com/services/qt_training.shtml Book • *Leading with Questions*	• When? Time frame? • With whom? • How? • Resources needed? • How communicated? • How to determine if at desired level?

Setting Goals and Expectations

Areas for Improvement (circle those you would like to develop)	Resources and Strategies	Action Plan
• Knowledge of SMART goals • Building mutually supported goals • Writing of goals	Chapter 7 resources • *Mentor-Mentee Agreement* • *Monitoring the Quality of the Mentor-Mentee Interactions* • *Mentoring Capabilities, Interests, and Resources* • *Worksheet for Evaluating Mentee's SMART Goals* • *Feedback Checklist* • *Assessing the Relationship with the Mentee* • *Initial Session with Mentee* Web site • http://humanresources.about.com/od/perfmeasurement/ Book • *Make Success Measurable! A Mindbook-Workbook for Setting Goals and Taking Action*	• When? Time frame? • With whom? • How? • Resources needed? • How communicated? • How to determine if at desired level?

Managing Differences

Areas for Improvement (circle those you would like to develop)	Resources and Strategies	Action Plan
• Self-awareness (attitudes, behavior) • Keeping discourse open and progressive • Understand conflict dynamics	Chapter 7 resources • *Exercises for Improving the Skill of Managing Differences* • *Improving Your Skill in Managing Differences* • *Monitoring the Quality of the Mentor-Mentee Interactions* Web sites • http://www.typelogic.com/typelinks.shtml • http://www.conflictdynamics.org/effectiveness_study.shtml • http://www.mapnp.org/library/org_chng/org_chng.htm	• When? Time frame? • With whom? • How? • Resources needed? • How communicated? • How to determine if at desired level?

Building Relationships and Environment

Areas for Improvement (circle those you would like to develop)	Resources and Strategies	Action Plan
• Physical setting and atmosphere • Making other person at ease • Communicating without fear • Nonverbal • Culture	Chapter 7 resources • *Mentor-Mentee Agreement* • *Monitoring the Quality of the Mentor-Mentee Interactions* • *Postsession Reflection for the Mentee* Book • *Driving Fear Out of the Workplace: Creating the High-Trust, High-Performance Organization*	• When? Time frame? • With whom? • How? • Resources needed? • How communicated? • How to determine if at desired level?

Problem Solving

Areas for Improvement (circle those you would like to develop)	Resources and Strategies	Action Plan
• Holistic problem solving • Action learning • Systems thinking • Creativity • Decision-Making	Chapter 7 resources • *Checklist for Problem Solving* • *Action Learning* Web sites • http://www.winstonbrill.com/index.html • http://www.mapnp.org/library/prsn_prd/decision.htm Books • *Solving Tough Problems: An Open Way of Talking, Listening, and Creating New Realities* • *Smart Questions: Learn How to Ask the Right Questions for Powerful Results*	• When? Time frame? • With whom? • How? • Resources needed? • How communicated? • How to determine if at desired level?

Managing Change

Areas for Improvement (circle those you would like to develop)	Resources and Strategies	Action Plan
• Become more comfortable with change • Improve change agent skills • Help others manage change	Chapter 7 resources • *Managing Change—Self-Study Exercises* • *Improving Your Skill in Managing Change* Web site • Overview of Organizational Change Book • *Leading Change*	• When? Time frame? • With whom? • How? • Resources needed? • How communicated? • How to determine if at desired level?

Understanding and Commitment to Learning

Areas for Improvement (circle those you would like to develop)	Resources and Strategies	Action Plan
• Action learning • Schools of learning • Andragogy • Project management • Reward and motivation • Questioning	Chapter 7 resources • *Mentoring Capabilities, Interests, and Resources* • *Learnings and Reflections at Mentoring Sessions* • *Action Learning* • *Learning/Reflection Exercise* • *Adult Learning Principles and Mentoring* • *Initial Session with Mentee* Web site • http://agelesslearner.com/intros/adultlearning.html Books • *Understanding and Facilitating Adult Learning: A Comprehensive Analysis of Principles and Effective Practices* • *The Adult Learner: The Definitive Classic in Adult Education and Human Resource Development (5th ed.)*	• When? Time frame? • With whom? • How? • Resources needed? • How communicated? • How to determine if at desired level?

Facilitation

Areas for Improvement (circle those you would like to develop)	Resources and Strategies	Action Plan
• Logistics management • Facilitation skills • Virtuality • Technology	Chapter 7 resources • *Learning and Reflections at Mentoring Sessions* Web site • www.mapnp.org/library/grp_skll/resource.htm Book • *The Skilled Facilitator*	• When? Time frame? • With whom? • How? • Resources needed? • How communicated? • How to determine if at desired level?

Analytical/Systems Thinking

Areas for Improvement (circle those you would like to develop)	Resources and Strategies	Action Plan
• Systems thinking • Analytical thinking • Creativity • Connecting action and learning • Openness	Chapter 7 resources • *Action Learning* Web sites • http://www.thinking.net/Systems_ Thinking/systems-thinking.htm • http://www.systemdynamics.org • http://www.sgzz.ch/links/stp/index.html • http://world.std.com/~lo/ • http://www.outsights.com/systems/welcome.htm • http://www.outsights.com/systems/arch/arch.htm • http://www.std.com/vensim/SDMAIL.HTM • http://web.mit.edu/sdg/www/ • http://www-leland.stanford.edu/group/SLOW/ Book • *Systems Thinking: Managing Chaos and Complexity*	• When? Time frame? • With whom? • How? • Resources needed? • How communicated? • How to determine if at desired level?

Reflection/Feedback

Areas for Improvement (circle those you would like to develop)	Resources and Strategies	Action Plan
• Feedback style • Timing of feedback • How to provide feedback • Listening	Chapter 7 resources • *Tips for Managers for Providing Feedback* • *Monitoring the Quality of the Mentor-Mentee Interactions* • *Feedback Checklist* • *Learning and Reflections at Mentoring Sessions* • *Postsession Reflection for the Mentee* • *Action Learning* Web site • www.mentoringgroup.com Book • *Feedback Toolkit: 16 Tools for Better Communication in the Workplace*	• When? Time frame? • With whom? • How? • Resources needed? • How communicated? • How to determine if at desired level?

Advocacy

Areas for Improvement (circle those you would like to develop)	Resources and Strategies	Action Plan
• Networking • Helping others to learn and grow • Model an appreciation of learning • Boosting confidence of others	Chapter 7 resources • *Exercises for Improving Advocacy Skills* • *Effective Advocacy Skills* • *Mentoring Capabilities, Interests, and Resources* • *Determining Mentor Readiness to Begin the Mentoring* Web site • http://www.score.org/business_tips.html	• When? Time frame? • With whom? • How? • Resources needed? • How communicated? • How to determine if at desired level?

Now that you have developed an action plan and identified strategies for the specific skills and attributes, it may be valuable to create an overall action plan in which you incorporate and integrate the individual plans developed previously.

Overall Action Plan

Skills and Attributes that I Have Chosen for My Action Plan	Resources and Strategies that I Will Be Using	Action Plan
		• When? Time frame?
		• With whom?
		• How?
		• Resources needed?
		• How communicated?
		• How to determine if at desired level?

NEXT STEPS

Managers and mentors develop and improve their skills through action and reflection. They become balanced, open, curious, and courageous, for example, by trying to be these things and by reflecting on their progress. The image of the wise guru on top of the hill can be misleading. The guru did not grow up on top of the hill, but rather through persistence, dedication, action, and reflection she developed her character, values, and skills. The image of the hill signifies that she is now dwelling in the results of her lifelong efforts and is able to be a resource to others.

How do mentors know that they are progressing? First they need to know where they want to go. A mentor who is not sure of his basic personality tendencies or orientations might benefit from taking the Myers-Briggs Type Indicator or other similar assessment tool as a way to identify areas that already position him for mentoring and other areas that may need development. One such assessment tool that a manager can take in just 10 or 15 minutes is the Jung Typology Test at HumanMetrics at http://www.humanmetrics.com/cgi-win/JTypes2.asp.

Technical University of Berlin and the European Academy for Women in Politics and Economics have an innovative program called Preparing Women to Lead. Qualified university graduates take part in internships in Germany, Belgium, Austria, and the Netherlands. For an intense three months, the women are paired with outstanding female mentors who teach them about the mentors' fields and management styles, organizational structures, processes of decision making, and the day-to-day requirements of management.[1]

Second, the mentor should understand that his potential for development is a mirror image of the mentee's development. The very indicators that a mentee is making progress should mark the development of the mentor as well. These include, for example:

- understanding appropriate behavior in social situations,
- understanding the organizational culture,
- developing an open flexible attitude,
- understanding different and conflicting ideas,
- becoming aware of organizational politics,
- developing personally,
- adjusting to change, and
- developing values.

As managers engage in mentoring, they can ask themselves a range of questions to help them reflect on their skills. As they record the answers to these questions in their journals, they can track their own progress. Examples of questions a mentor may ask include:

- Do I engage the mentee in nonjudgmental discussions?
- Do I use appropriate language (nonsexist, nonracist, nontechnical, nonjargon)?
- Do I encourage the mentee to develop her own responses rather than advise directly on what she should do?
- Do I provide the mentee with options?

- Do I set an example with ethical and professional behavior and demonstrate personal integrity?
- Do I show concern for the mentee's welfare?
- Do I work with the mentee to define the parameters of the mentoring relationship, being clear about what is and is not being offered?
- Do I use a flexible, open, and confident style?
- Do I listen carefully and ask open questions that evoke responses?
- Do I encourage, accept, and reinforce the mentee's expression of feelings, perceptions, concerns, beliefs, and suggestions?
- Am I clear, articulate, and direct in my communication?
- Do I encourage the mentee to establish goals and milestones to work toward, within, and beyond the mentoring relationship?
- Do I refer my mentee to other sources of information?
- Do I develop a feeling of trust and intimacy between myself and my mentee?
- Do I ask questions to help the mentee think about new possibilities?
- Do I suggest journals the mentee may be interested in reading or Web sites of interest?

In addition to improving self-awareness and attitudes toward mentoring, a manager can improve his or her functioning in the skills required for effective mentoring: listening, questioning, setting goals and expectations, managing differences, building relationships and environment, problem solving, managing change, understanding and commitment to learning, facilitation, analytical and systemic thinking, reflection and feedback, and advocacy.

Chapter 7 should already be familiar because you would have referred to various tools and instruments in that chapter in developing your action plans and choosing your strategies. Chapter 8 will provide annotated descriptions of valuable books and Web sites to assist you in building the skills and attributes of the effective and successful mentor.

SEVEN

Tools and Resources for Developing and Assisting the Manager/Mentor

In chapter 6, we asked you to identify the specific strategies and actions that would enable you as a manager to develop your mentoring capabilities. In this chapter, we provide a number of tools (including worksheets and exercises) and resources that can be utilized in your action plans. Many of the instruments and tools included in the following pages can be used to build more than one of the mentoring skills. The materials contained in this chapter can be used by the manager/mentor to (1) assist himself or herself and/or (2) assist the mentee.

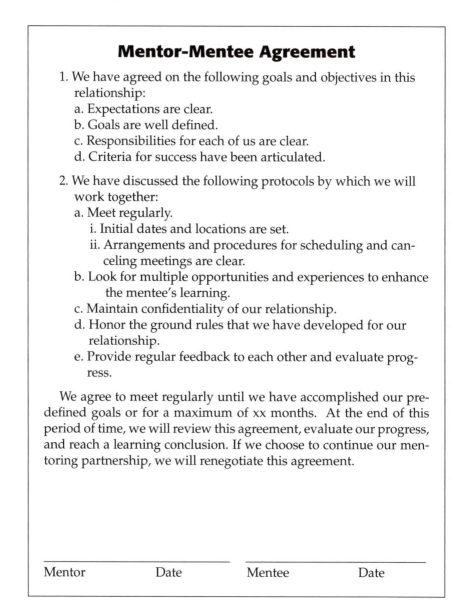

Mentor-Mentee Agreement

1. We have agreed on the following goals and objectives in this relationship:
   a. Expectations are clear.
   b. Goals are well defined.
   c. Responsibilities for each of us are clear.
   d. Criteria for success have been articulated.

2. We have discussed the following protocols by which we will work together:
   a. Meet regularly.
      i. Initial dates and locations are set.
      ii. Arrangements and procedures for scheduling and canceling meetings are clear.
   b. Look for multiple opportunities and experiences to enhance the mentee's learning.
   c. Maintain confidentiality of our relationship.
   d. Honor the ground rules that we have developed for our relationship.
   e. Provide regular feedback to each other and evaluate progress.

We agree to meet regularly until we have accomplished our predefined goals or for a maximum of xx months. At the end of this period of time, we will review this agreement, evaluate our progress, and reach a learning conclusion. If we choose to continue our mentoring partnership, we will renegotiate this agreement.

_____   _____

Mentor   Date   Mentee   Date

Monitoring the Quality of the Mentor-Mentee Interactions

Instructions: Complete the following form to guide you in your mentoring relationship. You might consider having the mentee fill out a similar form and then use both forms as a basis for discussion and improving the relations and power of the mentoring experience.

1. What have worked best so far in the interactions?

2. What could be improved?

3. What are the key learnings thus far?

4. In what ways are your learning goals being met?

5. In what ways are your learning needs not being met?

6. What might we do to make the mentoring process work better for us?

7. What has been your greatest learning success thus far?

8. Are the frequency and duration of the sessions adequate?

9. Other comments:

Mentoring Capabilities, Interests, and Resources

1. What are your strengths as a mentor?

2. Are you able to define the different roles that mentors play and your comfort level with each role?

3. What are the special and valuable resources that you are able to offer to the mentee?

4. How will you make the mentoring experience a successful learning process?

5. Do you know how to recognize when the mentoring is going off track and not working?

6. How will you bring the learnings and actions of this mentoring experience to others in the organization?

Feedback Checklist

My feedback

a. Would you like me to give you feedback on my observations?

b. Here is what I am seeing:

c. Here's how I see you progressing toward your goals:

d. Here are some suggestions for the future:

Exploring the Effect of my Feedback

a. How does my feedback connect with your perceptions?

b. Are my expectations realistic and helpful?

c. What further type of feedback would you like?

Feedback on your Learnings

a. What have you learned from my questions and observations?

b. What would you do differently?

c. What will you do now?

d. What are you learning?

e. What will you do differently as a result of this experience?

JUDGING VERSUS LEARNING
MIND-SET FOR ASKING QUESTIONS

Goldberg emphasizes how our mind-set frames how we see the world. It simultaneously programs what we believe to be our personal limitations as well as our possibilities.[1] Mind-sets define the parameters of our actions and interactions and affect, either explicitly or implicitly, outcomes in any area of focus. They are a determinant in deciding the types of questions we ask ourselves and others. In addition, one's mind-set determines how we observe, understand, and accept ourselves and others.

Goldberg refers to two types of mind-sets that may reside in the questioner: (1) learner and (2) judger.[2] In the learner mind-set, the questioner seeks to be responsive to life's circumstances. Thus, she is more likely to think objectively and strategically. The manager with a learner mind-set constantly searches for and creates solutions and relates to others in a win-win manner. Managers with the learning mind-set tend to be more optimistic and presuppose new possibilities, a hopeful future, and sufficient resources. They exude optimism, possibilities, and hope. They are thoughtful, flexible, and accepting. Such managers employ relationships that operate in a collaborative and innovative mode. A manager with the learner mind-set encourages and prepares workers to be more flexible, more open to new possibilities, and less attached to one's opinions and the need to be right. Such a manager seeks to strengthen subordinates' abilities to be conscious of their choices and responsible for their thoughts, feelings, behaviors, and outcomes.

According to Goldberg, the learning mind-set leads to much greater effectiveness, breakthroughs, and transformations. Although it is may be sometimes more difficult and challenging to operate within a learner mind-set, it is much more rewarding for everyone involved. Learning mind-sets lead to thinking objectively, creating solutions, and relating in a win-win way. Managers with learner mind-sets ask genuine questions, that is, questions to which they do not already know the answers. A learning mind-set presupposes fresh possibilities, a positive future, and abundant resources.

The judging mind-set, on the other hand, is reactive. It leads to over-emotional thinking and behavior. Managers with the judging mind-set tend to be more automatic and absolute in their actions; they emphasize negativity, pessimism, stress, and limited possibilities. The focus is more on problems than on solutions. Judging questions are inflexible and judgmental. For the judger, questions are more likely to be reactive to the situation and thereby lead to automatic reactions, limitations, and negativity. Judging questions result in win-lose relating as they all too often oper-

Table 7.1
Judge versus Learner Mind-Set

Judger Mind-Set	*Learner Mind-Set*
React to thoughts, feelings, situations, and other people	Responds to thoughts, feelings, situations, and other people
Automatic	Thoughtful
Knows-it-already mind-set	Beginner's mind-set
Judgmental, biased evaluation (standard: own belief and opinion)	Unbiased observer, researcher, and reporter (standard: truth, usefulness)
Win-lose relating	Win-win relating
Rigid, inflexible	Flexible
Thinks in terms of either or (right vs. wrong, good vs. evil)	Thinks in terms of both/and
Looks only from own point of view	Looks from multiple perspectives
Often only problem focused	Solution focused
Oriented toward rejection, defense, and/or attachment	Oriented toward acceptance, negotiation, teaming, and growth
Rarely takes responsibility for own thoughts, feelings, and actions	Takes responsibility for own thoughts, feelings, and actions
Assumes resources are scarce	Assumes resources are sufficient
Assumes possibilities are limited	Assumes possibilities are unlimited
Considers changes dangerous and resists it	Accepts change as constant and embraces it
Unaccepting and intolerant of self and others (especially "imperfections"	Accepting and tolerant of self and others
Operates in "attach-or-defend" mode	Operates in open, resolution-and-innovation-seeking mode

ate in an "attack or defend" paradigm. Such questioners often deny self-responsibility and search for other people or circumstances for blame. Managers with the judging mentality believe they know the answers already anyway. Table 7.1 summarizes these two divergent mind-sets that, in turn, result in totally different questions and questioning styles on the part of the manager.

Some examples of questions asked from the learning mind-set, according to Goldberg, include:

- What's good or useful about this circumstance?
- What possibilities does this situation open up?

- What can we do about this?
- How can we stay on track?
- What can we learn from this?[3]

Examples of judging questions, on the other hand, include:

- Why is this a failure?
- What's wrong with you?
- Whose fault is it?
- Why can't you get it right?[4]

By asking learning questions instead of judging questions, managers become more open to new possibilities and less attached to their opinions and a need to be right. They also experience a greater sense of personal responsibility for their thoughts, feelings, choices, and the outcomes that result from their actions.

Table 7.2
Tips for Mentors in Providing Feedback

What to Do	How to Do It	Examples
1. Align your feedback with the action and learning goals of the mentee	• Provide real-time feedback • Make it usable and realistic • Offer concrete and practical steps and options	• "I have a few ideas that might help …" • "What works for me is …"
2. Provide feedback about behavior that the mentee can do something about	• Focus on describing the behavior and examining possible ways of changing the behavior • Be specific rather than general	• "Are you aware of this behavior?" • "How to you think someone else might feel about that behavior?"
3. Seek to discuss from the perspective of the mentee	• Acknowledge that you are attempting to see context and situation as closely to the mentee's perspective as you can	• "Here is how I viewed or handled that situation …" • "How is your experience or perspective different from mine?"
4. Check out whether you understand what the mentee is saying	• Listen actively • Clarify and summarize • Ask questions	• "Is this what you are saying?" • "I understand that this was your experience or learning. Am I correct?"
5. Use a tone of respect	• Show interest • Demonstrate value in the mentee and her experience	• "I liked the way …" • "That seemed like a valuable learning or insight. Tell me more."
6. Be aware of your communication, management, and learning style	• Share and discuss your approach to learning and management	• "When this happens to me, this is how I tend to act." • "I enjoy …" • "I am uncomfortable when …"
7. Avoid giving feedback when you lack adequate information	• Take the time to acquire the information you need • Ask more questions	• "Could you give me more information before I give you my opinion?" • "I need to reflect on that some more. May I give my thoughts at our next session?"
8. Encourage learning from difficulties and mistakes	• Continuously link progress and learning to the big picture	• "How can you apply this?" • "What has been your most significant learnings thus far?"

Learning and Reflections
at Mentoring Sessions

1. How would you evaluate your experience from this assignment?

2. How would you rate yourself and your performance?

3. What have you accomplished?

4. What major problems did you experience and how did you overcome them?

5. How much self-direction did you exert and how much outside direction did you seek?

6. What were the most successful parts of the project?

7. How were you able to make it successful?

8. What surprised you most on this assignment?

9. What have you learned about yourself and how you work and learn?

10. How satisfied are you with the results and the learning?

11. What would you repeat next time?

12. What would you do differently?

13. What skills are you developing?

14. What preparations are you making for assuring success on this project?

Postsession Reflection for the Mentee

1. What went best at this session?

2. What actions did we agree to?

3. What learnings did we identify?

4. What was the quality of our communications and interaction?

5. How could we improve our mentoring relationship?

Assessing the Relationship with the Mentee

1. Am I providing adequate support to facilitate the learning of my mentee?

2. Have we identified sufficient and varied opportunities and venues for learning?

3. Are we continuing to build and maintain a productive relationship?

4. Is the quality of mentoring interaction satisfactory?

5. Have we put in place mechanisms to ensure continuous feedback?

6. Is the feedback I am giving thoughtful, candid, and constructive?

7. What am I learning as a mentor?

8. How can I apply these learnings?

Initial Session with the Mentee

Introductions

a. What knowledge, skills, and abilities I possess that might most benefit you:

b. What special learning or improvement opportunities I could provide:

Questions to ask Mentee?

a. Why do you want a mentor?

b. What experiences, knowledge, capabilities to you bring to the mentoring experience?

c. What are your short-term and long-term objectives?

d. How do you learn best?

Developing the Agreement

a. What should be the specific goals of our mentoring relationship?

b. How often should we meet?

c. What will be the best way I can be of help to you?
    i. advice
    ii. training
    iii. apprenticeship
    iv. sharing experiences
    v. a sounding board
    vi. coaching
    vii. connections
    viii. pathfinding
    ix. assignments
    x. other

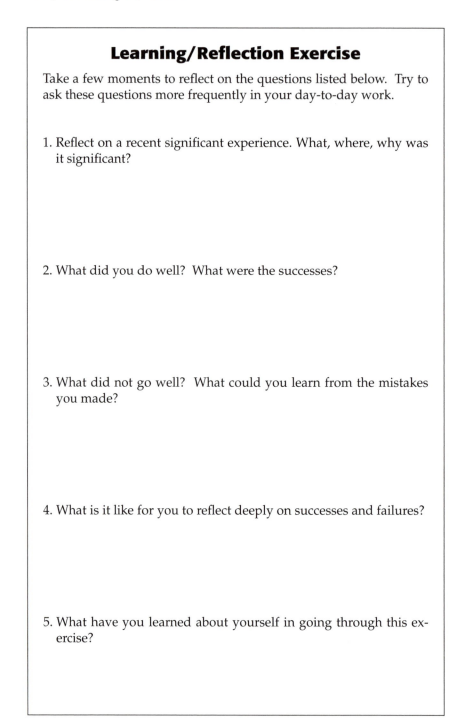

Learning/Reflection Exercise

Take a few moments to reflect on the questions listed below. Try to ask these questions more frequently in your day-to-day work.

1. Reflect on a recent significant experience. What, where, why was it significant?

2. What did you do well? What were the successes?

3. What did not go well? What could you learn from the mistakes you made?

4. What is it like for you to reflect deeply on successes and failures?

5. What have you learned about yourself in going through this exercise?

Table 7.3
Adult Learning Principles and Mentoring

Mentoring Element	Focus of the Mentor	Adult Learning Principles
Mentor role	A partner, coach, teacher, facilitator	Emphasis on the learning; focus on creating a supportive learning climate
Mentee role	Mentor and mentee equally responsible for managing the mentoring experience	Adults learn more effectively when they are involved in the diagnosis, planning, implementing, and assessment of their own learning
Learning process	Mentee directs and guides the mentoring process	Adult learners learn what is most valuable when they self-direct their learning
Length of relationship	Focus moves from calendar-based to goal-based	Readiness and intensity for learning increases when clear purpose and time
Setting	Not only face-to-face but also multiple and varied settings and situations	Learning can occur in a variety of settings; adult learners benefit from immediate application of the learning
Focus	Include both knowledge and the learning process itself	Learning how to learn and being internally motivated to learn

Checklist Questions for Problem Solving

Discovering and Sharing the Problem

a. Briefly describe the problem.

b. What is the history?

c. How long has it been a problem?

d. What part did you play in the problem?

e. Why is it a problem?

f. What do you believe is the real problem?

g. What are the costs of the problem?

Holistic Problem Solving

a. What are the desired possible solutions?

b. What are the obstacles?

c. How can you overcome those obstacles?

d. Who has the knowledge necessary?

e. Who has the passion to help solve this problem?

f. Who has the power to implement strategies?

Worksheet for Evaluating
the Mentee's SMART Goals

Specific

Are the goals specific, concrete, and clear?

Measurable

Are the goals measurable?

In what ways can the goals be measured?

Action Oriented

What specific actions will occur as a result of achieving the goals?

Realistic

Are the goals achievable in the time frame?

Timely

Has a completion date been set for attaining the goals?

Is the time allocated for accomplishing the goals reasonable?

Determining Mentor Readiness to Begin the Mentoring

(adapted from the *Mentor's Guide*, p. 92)

Yes   No

1. I have a sincere interest in helping the mentee succeed.

2. There appears to be mutual interest and compatibility.

3. Our assumptions about the mentoring process and the relationship are congruent.

4. I am clear about my role.

5. I believe that I am the right person to help the mentee achieve his goals.

6. I can enthusiastically engage in helping this person.

7. I am willing to use my network of contacts to help this person.

8. I can commit the necessary time to mentor this person.

9. I have access to resources that can support the mentee's learning.

10. I have the support that I need to be able to engage in this mentoring relationship in a valuable way.

11. I am committed to developing my mentoring skills.

12. I have a mentoring development plan in place.

SYNOPSIS: ACTION LEARNING

Since Reg Revans first introduced action learning in the coal mines of Wales and England in the 1940s, multiple variations of the concept have evolved, but all forms of action learning share the elements of real people resolving and taking action on real problems in real time and learning as they do so. The power and benefits of action learning are optimized when it integrates the following six components:

1. A Problem (Project, Challenge, Opportunity, Issue, or Task)

Action learning centers around a problem, project, challenge, issue, or task, the resolution of which is of high importance to an individual, team, and/or organization. The problem should be significant, urgent, and be the responsibility of the team to solve. It should also provide an opportunity for the group to generate learning opportunities, to build knowledge, and to develop individual, team, and organizational skills. Groups may focus on a single problem of the organization or multiple problems introduced by individual group members.

2. An Action-Learning Group or Team

The core entity in action learning is the action-learning group, which ideally is composed of four to eight individuals who have a diversity of backgrounds and experiences. These differences enable the group to see the problem or task from a variety of perspectives and thus allow the group's members to offer fresh and innovative viewpoints. Depending upon the action-learning problem, groups may be volunteers or may be appointed, may be from various functions or departments, may include individuals from other organizations or professions, and may involve suppliers as well as customers.

3. A Process that Emphasizes Insightful Questioning and Reflective Listening

Action learning emphasizes questions and reflection above statements and opinions. By focusing on the right questions rather than the right answers, action learning focuses primarily on what one does not know rather than on what one does know. Action learning tackles problems through a process of first asking questions to clarify the exact nature of the problem, reflecting and identifying possible solutions, and only then moving toward consideration of strategies and possible action. Questions prevent the group from solving the wrong problem and precipitously jumping into wrong action. In addition, the reflective inquiry process of action learning builds group cohesiveness, generates systems thinking, introduces innovative strategies, and generates individual and team learning.

4. Taking Action on the Problem

Members of the action-learning group must have the power to take action themselves or be assured that their recommendations will be implemented. If the group only makes recommendations, it looses its energy, creativity, and commitment. Likewise, no real, meaningful, or practical learning takes place until action is taken and reflected upon, for one is never sure an idea or plan will be effective until it has been implemented. Reflecting on action taken provides the best source for learning and organizational change.

5. A Commitment to Learning

Solving an organizational problem provides immediate, short-term benefits to the company. The greater, longer-term, multiplier benefit, however, occurs when the learnings gained by each group member as well as the group as a whole are applied strategically throughout the organization. Accordingly, action learning places as much emphasis on the learning and development of individuals and the team as it does on the solving of problems; the smarter the group becomes, the quicker and better will be the quality of its decision making and action taking.

6. An Action-Learning Coach

As other members of the group focus on solving the problem, one member of the group, the action-learning coach, devotes all of his efforts toward helping the group learn. This person identifies opportunities that enable the group to improve its problem-solving and strategy-creation capacity. Experience shows that unless a person is dedicated to the learning, a group tends to put all of its time and energies on that which they consider to be urgent (i.e., the problem) and neglect that which is actually more important in the long term (i.e., the learnings). Through posing a series of questions, the coach enables group members to reflect on how they listen, how they may better frame the problem, how they give one another feedback, how they are planning and working, and what assumptions may be shaping their beliefs and actions. The coaching role may be rotated among members of the group or may be a person assigned to that role throughout the duration of the group's existence.

HOW DOES AN ACTION-LEARNING PROGRAM WORK?

Action-learning groups may meet for one time or several times, depending upon the complexity of the problem and the time available for its resolution. The action-learning session may take place for one entire day, for a few hours over a few days, or over several months. A group may handle one or many problems. Whatever the time frame, however, action learning generally operates along the following stages and procedures:

Formation of the Group

The group may be volunteers or appointed and may be working on a single organizational problem or one another's department's problems. The group will have a predetermined amount of time and sessions, or it may determine the time parameters at the first meeting.

Presentation of the Problem or Task to the Group

The problem is briefly presented to the group by the problem presenter, who may remain as a member of the group or withdraw and await the group's recommendations.

Reframing the Problem

After a series of questions, the group, often with the guidance of the action-learning coach, will reach a consensus as to the most critical and important problem that the group should work on and establish the crux of the problem, which may differ from the problem as originally presented.

Determining Goals

Once the key problem or issue has been identified, the group seeks consensus for the goal, the achievement of which would solve the reframed problem for the long term with positive rather than negative consequences on the individual, team, or organization.

Developing Action Strategies

Much of the time and energy of the group will be spent on identifying and pilot testing possible action strategies. Like the preceding stages of action learning, strategies are developed via reflective inquiry and dialogue.

Taking Action

Between action-learning sessions, the group as a whole as well as individual members collect information, identify the status of support, and implement the strategies developed and agreed to by the group.

Capturing Learnings

Throughout and at any point during the sessions, the action-learning coach may intervene to ask the group members questions that will enable them to clarify the problem, find ways to improve their performance as a group, and identify how their learnings can be applied to develop themselves, the team, and the organization.

THREE MAJOR BENEFITS OF ACTION LEARNING

Action learning has the amazing capacity to simultaneously and effectively enable organizations to (1) solve complex, urgent problems; (2) develop skilled leaders; and (3) quickly build high-performing teams.

Solving Problems

Action learning begins and builds around solving problems; the more complex and the more urgent the problem, the better suited is the action learning methodology. The dynamic interactive process used in action learning allows the group to see problems in new ways and to gain fresh perspectives on how to resolve them. The action-learning process enables the group to look for underlying causes and leveraged actions rather than symptoms and short-term solutions. Action learning examines both macro- and microviews so as to discover when and how to best implement the proposed actions. As a result of its fresh approach to problem solving, action learning typically generates "breakthrough" insights, solutions, and effective strategies.

Leadership Development

Most leadership development programs, whether corporate or academic, are ineffective and expensive. Teachers rather than practitioners are the source of knowledge. Because the business environment is changing so fast, the knowledge gained in the classroom is out-of-date, and little, if any, of the knowledge ever gets transferred to the workplace. In addition, executive development programs provide little of the social and interpersonal aspects of real-life organizations and tend to focus on tactical rather than strategic leadership.

Action learning differs from normal leadership training in that its primary objective is to ask appropriate questions in conditions of risk rather than to find answers that have already been precisely defined by others. Action learning does not isolate any dimension from the context in which managers work; rather it develops the whole leader for the whole organization. What leaders learn and how they learn cannot be dissociated from each other, because how one learns necessarily influences what one learns.

Building Teams

Teams formed via the action-learning process quickly become both high performing and strongly bonded. Their effectiveness improves every time they meet because of the learnings built via the interventions of the action-learning coach. A unique ability to think and learn as a team steadily emerges as the group develops clearness, deep communications, and committed collaboration around strategies for which they are accountable.

WHY IS ACTION LEARNING SO POWERFUL?

What accounts for this marvelous power and value of action learning? Action learning works not because of luck but because it inherently interweaves a wide array of organizational, psychological, sociological, and educational theories and principles as well as key elements of ethics, political science, engineering, and systems thinking. Each of the six components reinforce and leverage the power of action learning. The simplicity and immediate applicability of action learning has enabled organizations around the world to achieve success in problem solving, team building, organizational learning, and leadership development.

Exercises for Essential Listening Skills

The following are three exercises anyone can use to practice good listening skills and become more self-aware of your listening style. (For more advanced listening practice, you may want to consider taking a workshop or working with an executive or shadow coach.)

Exercise 1

Think of three different people you talk to at work. For each, remember an actual conversation. For example, you could pick a controversy, a recurring discussion, or a crisis for your business as the subject of conversation. For each, run through the listening flowchart for at least four loops to see where the conversation might have gone if you had made different choices. Then run through the flowchart again, trying out a different series of choices.

Exercise 2

Choose someone you work with to whom you are comfortable talking. Ask for their help. Tell them you are trying to improve your listening skills. Get their permission to walk through the steps of the listening flowchart, or to experiment with recapping and asking nonleading questions, during some of your actual work-related conversations together.

Exercise 3

Experiment with your listening skills in casual conversations with friends or strangers you meet at social gatherings or with service providers who serve you in your nonbusiness capacity (for example, the manager at your favorite bookstore or auto repair shop).

ATTENTIVE LISTENING SKILLS

Attentive listening means thinking and acting in ways that connect you with the speaker. Although active listening usually happens naturally when we are very interested in what someone is saying, we can also choose to listen actively whenever we want to maximize the quality of our listening, both in terms of the effect it has on us and in terms of the effect it has on those we are speaking to. By contrast, when people multitask while someone speaks, they rarely listen effectively.

You can take several simple steps to improve your listening. The quality of information exchanged, your own experience as a listener, the experience of the person you are listening to, and your relationship with the listener will all benefit. The steps are:

1. Get over Yourself and Give Them a Solo

If you assert your own position at every opening in a conversation you will eliminate many of the potential benefits of listening. In particular, people you are talking with will not feel respected by you, their thinking and brainstorming will be inhibited, and they may even withhold important information out of caution or out of anger.

Wait until they finish making their points before you speak. Do not interrupt, even to agree with them, and do not jump in with your own suggestions before they explain what they have already done, plan to do, or have thought about doing. This includes being aware enough to stop yourself from doing any of the following:

- making critical or judgmental faces or sounds,
- trying to "fix" their problem with a quick suggestion,
- interrogating them to make them answer a question you have about their situation,
- trying to cheer them up or tell them things are not so bad,
- criticizing them for getting into their situation, and
- telling them what you would do or have done in the past.

All of these responses interrupt what they are saying or change the direction of the conversation before they have an opportunity to get to their point. The first thing people bring up when they have something to say often is not the central point they will eventually make, whether they know it or not. Listening carefully for a while first gives both the talker and the listener a chance to develop an understanding about what exactly the issue is. After you think they have reached a stopping point, you can ask something like "May I make a suggestion?" before you start to make sure they are ready to give up the floor.

2. Stop Multitasking

Do not multitask if you are supposed to be listening. You wind up listening only to part of what someone says or pretending to listen while you think about something else. You also sacrifice catching important nonverbal cues and information about their intent, their confidence level, and their commitment level. Even if you think that you can get enough of what people say while multitasking to serve your immediate purposes, you should assume as a general rule that people notice when you do not listen to them attentively.

If you are tempted to split your attention between listening and something else, ask yourself whether you can risk appearing disinterested and risk the negative impression that it is likely to make. Avoid allowing interruptions that cause you to lose concentration or split your attention. Eliminate background noise, ringing telephones, and people dropping in. Do not read e-mail, use a computer, or read something while someone else is talking to you.

3. Recap Regularly

Very skilled listeners practice and become good at recapping both the facts and the level of importance (the emotional drift of the speaker) in a few brief words. If you do not understand or are not sure about a point they are trying to make, repeat a very brief portion of the part you did not understand and ask them to tell you more about it to help you understand better.

4. Use Connecting Words

Where it helps, use words that show you are connecting with what they are saying, such as "Uh-huh," "OK," "Yeah," "I get it," and so forth.

5. Use Body Language

Use positive body language, such as making frequent eye contact and facing them squarely. Avoid negative body language, such as frowning and looking away. A great deal of research has been done about body language. Books have been written about it. Some people claim to be experts at interpreting it. But for the rest of us, it is enough to be aware that body language exists and to use it constructively when we can.

EFFECTIVE ADVOCACY SKILLS

Effective advocacy requires that managers have a keen sense of the value of developing staff and that the effort put into staff development

Exercises for Improving Advocacy Skills

Following are three exercises to better understand and improve your capacity to be an advocate.

1.   Review Wayne's idea about bringing Jocelyn to a senior staff meeting (chapter 2) and ask yourself the following questions:

- Am I comfortable with promoting inexperienced colleagues among my managerial peers, even to the extent of arranging for them to present their ideas or initiatives to senior staff?
- What does Wayne risk by bringing Jocelyn to the meeting with him? What does he stand to gain?
- What is the impact of taking employees' good ideas to senior staff meetings and presenting them as our own?
- Is Jocelyn likely to view Wayne as a more powerful or less powerful manager as a result of his taking her to the senior staff meeting?
- If Jocelyn performed poorly at the senior staff meeting, what responses might she expect from Wayne? What would be your responses in a similar situation?

2. Reflect on the job responsibilities of your employees and on the goals of your office/unit/organization. Then imagine what kind of learning would make your employees more capable, powerful, and motivated to achieve their and the organization's goals. Finally, identify books, videos, and training opportunities for your staff to improve their capabilities. Better yet, empower a team to carry out this initiative and be sure to encourage and support them at every opportunity.

3. Invite your fellow managers to establish a rotational internship program in which staff can spend up to one month working in another office, assigned a guide under the watchful eye of the office manager, and invited to reflect on organizational learning and communication issues. Ask participating staff to identify the best communication, empowerment, and learning practices that can be shared through the organization. Celebrate the accomplishments of participants at organization-wide meetings and reinforce their valuable contributions by incorporating some of their recommendations for enhancing communication and learning opportunities.

Exercises for Improving the Skill of Managing Differences

Following are three exercises to better understand and improve your capacity to manage differences/conflict.

1. Do you wonder whether you see yourself as others see you? Here is an exercise you can do that will help you discover how close are your and your colleagues' perceptions of your style. This exercise can also help you improve communications with your staff.

Create three or four common situations relating to managing differences/conflict in the workplace and write down how you would respond to each one. At a subsequent meeting with your staff, ask them to write down how they think you would respond in the same situations. Keep the exercise anonymous and be sure to let them know why you are asking their help. After you have a chance to process their responses and compare them with your self-perception, share the results with them and process the differences. Finally, identify areas that you want to change in yourself. Some examples of common situations in the workplace:

a. You pass by your program assistant and project officer who are having a heated discussion about who is responsible for coordinating the assembly of the annual plan. What would you most likely do in such a situation? (e.g., Intervene and ask whether you can help? Continue on, believing that they can work it out? Make a mental note to talk with each of them later?)

b. A person of the opposite gender comes into your office and confides to you that your deputy appears consistently to exhibit gender bias. How would you handle this situation? (e.g., Go to your deputy and ask him/her what is going on? Carefully question the person who confides in you to ascertain whether his/her observation is valid? Make time to chat with staff whose gender differs from your deputy's and sound them out about their observations?)

c. In a staff meeting, one of your employees challenges your position. What would you do?

2. Test your skills in managing diversity of opinion and attaining compromise in a staff meeting where a problem is being addressed. Through the use of questioning and reflection, elicit possible solutions from your staff and help them to become aware of and reflect on the reasons for their different positions. Then push toward problem resolution by asking questions such as: Among the potential solutions, which seem to hold the most promise? What will be the impact on us and on our clients in selecting one or another potential solution? Are there elements of each that appeal to all of us? Where can we find common ground? How are we going to compromise and come up with a solution we all can live with? Avoid making the decision yourself.

3. Review Wendy's concerns about Karl and her decision to confront him (chapters 1 and 2) and ask yourself the following questions: When I consider confronting someone, do I tend to think that one of us has to win and the other lose? What was Wendy willing to risk (give up) in order to help Karl look at his motivation and commitment to the mentoring relationship? Wendy feared/assumed that Karl might have issues with women. Do I have fears or assumptions that make me hesitant to act? How can I face these fears or assumptions?

will enhance organizational goals and increase the influence of the manager. The effective advocate is something like the proud parent who, realizing that her son or daughter is the future of the family, concentrates on helping her child to be an even better parent than she was.

Effective advocates open doors, make suggestions, celebrate successful efforts, and look for valuable lessons in failed efforts. Advocates do not strictly control their staff's actions but clear the path for them to excel. They question and challenge when staff make wrong turns, encouraging them to reflect on the impact of their choices and to consider all available options. Effective advocates give their staff progressively more responsible assignments, give them positive feedback, even using them as examples in the presence of others, and ask for their opinions and advice on matters outside of their realm of responsibility.

Successful advocates are positive people who expect great things from others and celebrate positive behavior and both small and large successes. They push their staff into the limelight, understanding that they, by empowering, will become even more powerful.

IMPROVING YOUR SKILL IN MANAGING
DIFFERENCES AND CONFLICT

What happens when a highly organized mentor has a mentee with a re-laxed work style? When a creative mentee has a mentor who tends to be linear in his thinking? When an assertive mentor has a somewhat passive mentee? Potential for frustration and conflict abound in mentoring relationships, and mentors should assess and develop their ability to manage conflict.

A recent survey by the Leadership Development Institute (LDI) at Eck-erd College found that nearly 70 percent of managers spend more than 10 percent of their time handling workplace conflict, and 44 percent of managers spend more than 20 percent of their time on conflict-related is-sues. Another LDI study found a link between a person's ability to resolve conflict and his or her perceived effectiveness as a leader.

Managers who manage differences well in their personal and work lives likely will be prepared for differences and conflicts that may arise in mentor-ing relationships. From time to time conflict may arise between mentors and mentees with respect to personality differences, expectations within the re-lationship, or level of commitment. The mentee may be a dependent person who expects the mentor to open doors for him. He may be abrasive, passive, or neglectful. A mentor does not want to come to scheduled meetings dreading a struggle or being resentful at his mentee's seeming lack of energy.

Managers who recognize, appreciate, and celebrate differences have a head start in managing conflict. Mangers who are comfortable with com-promise, who recognize that there are often many good solutions to work-place problems, and who are comfortable with fostering dialogue rather than debate are likely to be effective in managing differences and conflict. Ability to manage conflict can help the mentor to facilitate and be a role model for the mentee who experiences conflict in his work life outside of the mentoring relationship. Conflict management is a critical skill for managers, mentors, and leaders.

Cross-Cultural Mentoring at the Livermore National Laboratory

The Lawrence Livermore National Laboratory is a U.S. Department of Energy national laboratory operated by the University of California. Founded in 1952 as a nuclear weapons design laboratory, the lab also has become one of the world's premier scientific centers where cut-ting-edge science and engineering in the interest of national security is used to break new ground in other areas of national importance, including energy, biomedicine, and environmental science.

The lab recognized that to achieve its programmatic mission, it had to find ways to develop and keep a diverse pool of talent. This required careful attention to hiring, career development, mentoring, and continued education. The lab's Cross-Cultural Mentoring Program, offered by the Affirmative Action & Diversity Program, was created in 1994 to foster career growth, develop leadership skills, increase the effectiveness of protégés, and broaden perspectives and increase awareness and sensitivity of cultural differences for both the mentor and mentee.

Mentors and mentees meet twice a month for approximately one year, though many of the partnerships remain active well beyond that period. Mentors and mentees are matched according to career aspirations, job position, function, and background, with a special emphasis on diversity.

The program provides opportunities for participants to explore diversity issues, to build self-confidence, and to learn about the various cultures of the lab. Mentees report that the biggest benefits from the program include:

- insight about unwritten rules and organizational culture,
- increased motivation,
- increased understanding of management thinking, and
- obtaining a long-term confidant and adviser for sensitive career issues.

Mentors also benefit by learning the values, expectations, and work styles of a new generation of employees; developing sensitivity to diversity; and broadening their perspectives on work-related issues. The program has heightened sensitivity of all participants to ways that institutions can be insensitive to certain groups of people and sharpened the ability to see things from another person's point of view.

Managing Change—Self-Study Exercises

Following are three exercises to better understand and improve your capacity to manage differences/conflict.

1. Reread Wendy's and Wayne's reflections on their mentoring experiences (chapter 4) and reflect on the following questions: How did Wayne's attitude about mentoring change after he became involved as a mentor? What was the impact of Wayne's mentee on his behavior as a manager? Overall, what kind of changes did mentoring engender in Wayne and his staff?

2. Take a few moments to identify those in your organization whom you consider to be change agents. List their qualities, habits, typical behaviors. Are they risk takers? Are they people-oriented? Are they respectful? Are they consensus seekers? Do they have a broad vision for the organization? Which of their qualities are most related to their success as change agents?

3. Administer a brief Likert survey at a staff meeting, using Fullan and Miles's (1992) principles of change. Use the indicators: strongly agree, agree, neutral, disagree, strongly disagree:

1. Change is learning, loaded with uncertainty.
2. Change is a journey, not a blueprint.
3. Problems are our friends.
4. Change is resource-hungry.
5. Change requires the power to manage it.
6. Change is systemic.
7. All large-scale change is implemented locally.

Process the responses immediately, asking staff why they answered as they did. Ask staff how they feel about change and what changes they have noted recently in the workplace. Ask them for ideas about how the unit as a whole should manage change. As they share ideas and feelings, make note of those who display resistance to change, indifference, and receptivity so that you will have a better idea of how to manage change with your staff.

IMPROVING YOUR SKILL IN MANAGING CHANGE

Organizational culture comprises shared history, values, and beliefs and common attitudes and behavior. Change can create a new culture, combine cultures, or reinforce cultures. Understanding a company's culture is helpful in managing internal change and that which originates in the larger culture. Here are some tips for managers who facilitate the change process. Use a systems or holistic approach to ensure that all organizational elements are considered when planning and implementing change.

1. Make use of teams and involve all stakeholders in the change process.
2. Empower others to implement changes.
3. Recognize that you are in an environment of flux, that the changes you initiate will not bring the organization to a period of lengthy stability.
4. Remember that the most important agents of change are people. Pay attention to staff feelings about change and provide ample time to process them.
5. Be prepared for the trauma that change can bring and for the possibility that things may worsen before change is embraced.
6. Recognize your natural allies among those who are open to change, but do not abandon those who are resistant or who need more time.

Managers who are adept at team building are likely to be successful at managing change. Leaders who can challenge, motivate, and empower their staff through change will be effective change agents. Change tends to undermine teamwork, and managers who can keep their work teams focused during changes will keep their organizations and businesses healthy.

Based on your experiences as both manager and mentor, you should increase your tolerance for ambiguity, for risk, and for conflict. You should become more comfortable with a broad vision and with an open systems focus. To help your employees be prepared for and embrace change, you should provide opportunities for them to keep their knowledge and skills current. You should model a flexible attitude toward chaos and reduced job security even while giving employees the message that their creativity, learning, and development are the only stable factors in the global economy.

ADDITIONAL RESOURCES

In chapter 8, we present a wide array of additional resources found on the Internet as well as the best books in the field of mentoring and on the various skills of mentoring.

EIGHT

Resources for
the Manager as Mentor

Mentoring has become an immensely important subject around the world. Amazon.com lists nearly 1,000 books dealing with the topic *mentor*. More than 10 million Web sites are listed when *mentor* is typed into Google. Access to the purchase of a variety of books or to reading millions of pages of interesting and valuable information about mentoring can be very beneficial, although it is also overwhelming to the reader. To assist in determining which books and Web sites would be most useful to the manager/mentor, we have identified what we consider to be the most valuable resources. Of course, many more Web sites will be developed and more books will be published on mentoring, so the reader is advised to update the resources listed in this chapter. We will first present Web sites that discuss mentoring in general and then present Web sites that explore the mentoring skills and attributes discussed in the previous chapters of the book.

WEB SITES

Mentoring, General

Mentoring Group (http://www.mentoringgroup.com/home.html): The Mentoring Group is a division of the Coalition of Counseling Centers (CCC), founded in 1980 by Dr. Brian Jones, Dr. Linda Phillips-Jones, and colleagues in the San Francisco Bay area. The Web site offers the visitor a soup-to-nuts description of mentoring programs with insights and tips in the following areas:

- starting a program,
- improving a program,
- evaluation,
- best practices,
- ethics,
- personal vision,
- vision statement,
- development plan,
- reasons to be a mentor,
- research,
- vision, and
- development plan.

National Mentoring Partnership (http://www.mentoring.org): The National Mentoring Partnership (NMP) is an advocate for the expansion of mentoring and a resource for mentors and mentoring initiatives nationwide. The National Mentoring Partnership is dedicated to the expansion of quality mentoring. In NMP's vision:

- Entire communities and states work together to sustain and expand mentoring opportunities for young people.
- Schools, businesses, civic associations, faith communities, and youth-serving organizations build or strengthen their mentoring programs.
- Educators and workforce preparation leaders integrate mentoring into programs.
- Individuals learn about mentoring opportunities and become the mentors young people want and need.

The National Mentoring Partnership offers links to state mentoring partnerships, offers online training to brush up on mentoring skills, provides information on running a mentoring program, identifies written resources on mentoring, and offers an online "whiz quiz" on mentoring.

Peer Resources: Mentor Papers online (http://www.peer.ca/mentor-papers): Peer Resources (PR) offers a number of useful sources of information for managers and mentors:

1. PR scans the Internet for articles on mentoring and provides summaries and links to the originals.
2. PR also offers a searchable, annotated bibliography on mentoring.
3. PR offers a free online magazine (e-zine) The Mentor News (www.mentors.ca/thementornews.html). The publication examines trends, issues, and research and provides announcements regarding mentoring events and conferences as well as funding sources.

In some instances, access to full articles is limited to peer resources members (dues = $54 annually). To members, PR offers sample evaluation forms and surveys, mentor profile tools, mentor agreements, a list of matching tools, and program management systems. PR also has virtual mentors and other experts who provide information and support.

Mentoring Leadership Resource Network (http://www.mentors.net/03joinform.html): The Mentoring Leadership and Resource Network (MLRN) is a grassroots effort started by a few educators and supported, in part, as a network of the Association for Supervision and Curriculum Development. Though especially attentive to educators, MLRN offers many articles on models of mentoring, provides design of mentoring programs and training for mentors, and provides resources for mentoring programs. Membership is free.

Coaching & Mentoring Network (http://www.coachingnetwork.org.uk/Default.htm): The Coaching & Mentoring Network was established to provide a service both for people who provide coaching or mentoring services and for those seeking them. The network is primarily a Web-based service designed to serve people in both the business and broader communities. Among the resources available at the site are:

- Coaching and Mentoring Bookshop,
- articles from the press and electronic media,
- links to other Web sites offering related information and services,
- information on training programs,
- real case studies of coaching programs,
- events in the arena of coaching and mentoring, and
- news from the world of coaching and mentoring.

The network's offerings of articles and case studies are valuable practical helps to mentors and mentoring coordinators.

Strategic Planning and Action Plans

Community Tool Box for Developing Strategic and Action Plans (http://ctb.ku.edu/tools/developstrategicplan/index.jsp): The resource provides practical guidance on how to develop an action plan, including:

- outline for developing strategic and action plans,
- narrative outline (with links to how-to sections of the Community Tool Box),
- example(s) of strategic and action plans,
- how-to information on developing strategic and action plans,
- learning community on strategic planning—learning through online exchanges with others doing this work,
- other resources and links related to developing strategic and action plans, and
- quick tips and tools for doing this work.

Listening

Business Listening (http://www.businesslistening.com/): This is a reference site explaining the role of listening—and information derived from listening—in leadership, customer relationships, and persuasion (conflict resolution and negotiation). Features include articles by coaches, consultants, and other professionals; reviews, with analysis, of pertinent business literature; and self-training guides and exercises concerning listening strategy and skills.

Questioning

Center for Inquiring Leadership (http://www.inquiryinc.com/services/qt_training.shtml): The site provides information, training, and other services related to improving the questioning skills of managers. The Center for Inquiring Leadership (CIL) has a number of training programs designed to promote the expert application of inquiry and reflection skills by managers to themselves, others, and their organizations. The training programs seek to develop the following eight characteristics that CIL research shows to be important for inquiring leaders:

1. An insatiable, nonjudgmental curiosity in which leaders place a high value on continuous learning for themselves and others and model inquiry that is constructive rather than criticizing.
2. A commitment to establishing an inquiring culture (both formal and informal) in their organizations and/or teams, appreciating

that many people have some reluctance about asking questions and need to be encouraged to do so.

3. An ability to challenge assumptions and beliefs in thinking and communication, solicit honest feedback, and willingness to suspend their own opinions in the face of new data and to not know and not be right.

4. An ability to listen carefully and thoroughly, especially when not liking or agreeing with what they may be hearing. This includes questioning people about their opinions, perspectives, motivations, needs, and expectations.

5. A commitment to take *reflecting time* when formulating questions and answers and encourage others to do the same.

6. A commitment to institute standard, inquiry-based problem-solving and learning practices, especially those based on principles of action learning.

7. An ability to intentionally ask themselves and others questions that open thinking, challenge assumptions, and seek creative solutions, to think about their own thinking (and question their questions), to manage their thinking, feeling, and behaviors.

8. The strength to be decisive and committed to strategic rather than reactive action.

QuestionThinking (QT), the system of techniques at the heart of CIL's training programs for developing the inquiring leader, is based upon the following core premises:

- Thinking occurs as an internal question-and-answer process, regardless of whether the individual is aware of this. In other words, thoughts that are statements represent answers to preceding thoughts that are questions.

- These internal questions virtually program thoughts, feelings, behaviors, and outcomes, whether or not an individual is aware of having asked themselves those questions.

- One's internal questions are the key leverage for understanding mental models, uncovering assumptions, altering attitudes and patterns of interaction, and creating different results.

- Therefore, it is important to learn how to discern the questions being asked, utilize models for analyzing these questions for effectiveness, and develop skills to revise and re-ask the questions if better ones could lead to better results.

- Effective questions (either internal or interpersonal questions) lead to effective results, ineffective questions to ineffective results, missed or avoided questions to unpredictable (and sometimes problematic) results.

- Most people are barely aware of the existence, prevalence, relevance, or power of internal (or interpersonal) questions and therefore lack both the motivation and ability to take advantage of this naturally occurring cognitive and linguistic resource.
- QT (question-based strategic, creative, and tactical thinking) lives at the juncture of leadership, coaching, and action learning.

Setting Goals and Expectations

Performance Goal Setting and Performance Measurement (http:// humanresources.about.com/od/perfmeasurement): This Web site provides resources and articles on goal setting, assessments, and other human resources issues.

Managing Differences and Managing Change

Type Logic (http://www.typelogic.com/typelinks.shtml): This Web site offers links to sources of information and understanding about values important to managers and mentors. Here you can find links to information about your Myers-Briggs type indicator; you can even take the Jung Typology Test and Keirsey's Temperament Sorter II and have them assessed while you wait.

Other links explore personal growth of individuals in an organization or provide information about types under stress.

Conflict Dynamics (http://www.conflictdynamics.org/effectiveness_ study.shtml): The Conflict Dynamics Profile Web site is hosted by Eckerd College and offers insight into the behaviors people typically display when faced with conflict and into the potential for people to change their behavior for the better.

The profile focuses on four basic approaches to conflict:

1. Active-constructive:
   - perspective taking
   - creating solutions
   - reaching out
   - expressing emotions
2. Passive-constructive
   - reflective thinking
   - delay responding
   - adapting
3. Active-destructive
   - winning at all costs
   - displaying anger

- demeaning others
- retaliating
4. Passive-destructive
   - avoiding
   - yielding
   - hiding emotions
   - self-criticizing

The Web site offers links to other Web sites and books on building relationships, managing emotions, resolving conflict, accepting conflict, and hot buttons. If you want to know what sets you off, it also offers a hot-buttons test that you can take online.

Overview of Organizational Change (http://www.mapnp.org/library/org_chng/org_chng.htm): This Web site, assembled by Carter McNamara, offers an excellent reflection on the organizational change process and links to sites about strategic planning, organizational communications, organizational performance management, appreciative inquiry, communities of practice, and other topics. Also included are links to free management libraries, including a change management library.

Problem Solving

Winston Brill and Associates (http://www.winstonbrill.com/index.html): Winston Brill and Associates is a consulting and publishing company that focuses on creativity and innovation. This site offers access to hundreds of articles on creativity and innovation. A few examples of articles available include:

- "Techniques for Creative Thinking: Yes, They Work" by Gary A. Davis, Ph.D.
- "Effective Criticism Made Easy: Basic Rules for Delivering Negative Feedback to Others" by Robert A. Baron, Ph.D.
- "Creative Thinking—Make It a Habit!" by Jack Oliver, Ph.D.
- "Harvesting the Advantages of Cultural Diversity" by Rudolph J. Marcus, Ph.D.
- "Taking Advantage of Intuition" by Weston H. Agor, Ph.D.
- "Three Silly Notions about Technology Transfer: And One That's Not" by R. Stephen Berry, Ph.D.
- "New Product Development in Small and Large Companies" by Sandra S. Donovan, Ph.D.
- "Building a Winning Team" by David E. Gootnick and Margaret Mary Gootnick

Problem Solving (http://www.mapnp.org/library/prsn_prd/prob_slv.htm): Carter McNamara created this Web site that includes a vast array of information about and resources for problem solving. Includes suggested basic steps for problem solving, basic guidelines to problem solving and decision making, problem solving (includes some basic steps), and decision making and problem solving. The Web site offers tips for creative problem solving, leadership styles, and problem solving (with a focus on creativity), with 10 tips for beefing up problem solving. In-depth information is provided on topics such as:

appreciative inquiry,
problem-solving techniques (extensive overview of various approaches),
guidelines for selecting an appropriate problem-solving approach,
factors to consider in figuring out what to do about a problem,
structured development of problem-solving methods (somewhat advanced and abstract), and
a case for reengineering the problem-solving process (somewhat advanced).

The Web site also connects the reader to a large number of online discussion groups, newsletters (e-zines), and so forth in the overall areas of management, business, and organization development.

Systems Thinking

Systems Thinking (http://www.thinking.net/Systems_Thinking/systems_thinking.html): This Web site contains papers on systems thinking such as "Introduction to Systems Thinking" and "How Systems Thinking Can Improve the Results of Innovation Efforts."

System Dynamics Society (http://www.systemdynamics.org): This is the home page of the System Dynamics Society and includes a history of system dynamics, a brief description of its tools and applications, information about the annual system dynamics conference, and information on the *System Dynamics Review,* a refereed journal.

Systems Thinking Practice (http://www.sgzz.ch/links/stp/index.html): It provides a map of systems thinking, cybernetics, cognition, and other resources on the Web.

Learning Org Discussion Pages (http://world.std.com/~lo/): This is the home of the Learning-Org list, which has more than 1,400 members on several continents. Messages are organized by thread, date, and subject. You can participate in the Learning-Org list directly from these pages.

Mental Model Musings (http://www.outsights.com/systems/welcome.htm): This link will take you to an article that provides a good overview of the history, development, and principles of systems thinking. The site also offers additional links to other systems-thinking-related issues, such as the different systemic situations that appear frequently across disciplines. These are known as archetypes.

System Dynamics: Archetypes (http://www.outsights.com/systems/arch/arch.htm): This link takes you to a list of the systemic situations that appear frequently across disciplines, called archetypes.

System Dynamics Mailing List and Discussion Pages (http://www.std.com/vensim/SDMAIL.HTM): The site includes a mailing list and discussion group about system dynamics.

MIT System Dynamics Group (http://web.mit.edu/sdg/www/): In addition to information about the MIT System Dynamics Group and its publications, this page has links to the System Dynamics in Education Project and other resources about system-dynamics-based computer models.

Stanford Learning Organization Web (SLOW) (http://www.leland.stanford.edu/group/SLOW/): The Stanford Learning Organization Web contains further suggested readings, subscription information for their electronic discussion group on learning organizations, and links to other systems thinking sites.

Understanding and Commitment to Learning

How Adults Learn: Ageless Learner (http://agelesslearner.com/intros/adultlearning.html): This Web site provides interesting articles on adult learning as well as resources and links to other Web sites on the following topics:

andragogy and pedagogy,
learning styles assessment to help you identify your dominant learning style,
learning styles introduction puts learning styles information into easy-to-understand language and provides sources where you can learn more,
motivation style assessment to help identify what motivates you to learn, and
primer on educational psychology introduces you to the different ways schools and formal learning programs approach learners and materials to learn.

The Web site also discusses adult learning theories, principles, and best practices and includes recommendations for best books in adult learning.

Facilitation, Reflection, and Feedback

Resources for Facilitators (www.mapnp.org/library/grp_skll/re-source.htm): This Web site provides information and additional Web links on the following topics:

facilitation—learning about basics,
facilitating in face-to-face groups,
facilitating online groups (virtual communities),
feedback (giving and sharing),
focus groups,
group-based problem solving and decision making,
group dynamics,
group learning,
group performance management,
icebreakers and warm-up activities,
interviews (many kinds),
large-scale interventions,
listening,
meeting management,
nonverbal communications,
open-space technology,
presenting,
questioning,
self-directed and self-managed work teams,
team building, and
virtual teams.

The Web site also provides a list of organizations, libraries, and online groups that focus on the topic of facilitation.

Advocacy and Empowerment

SCORE (http://www.score.org/business_tips.html): SCORE's extensive national network of 10,500 retired and working volunteers are experienced entrepreneurs and corporate managers and executives. These volunteers provide free business counseling and advice as a public service to all types of businesses in all stages of development. SCORE is a resource partner with the U.S. Small Business Administration.

SCORE Counselors to America's Small Business provides entrepreneurs with free, confidential, face-to-face and online business counseling. Counseling and workshops are offered at 389 chapter offices nationwide by experienced business volunteers. Among SCORE's free services is leadership advice that is helpful to managers and mentors. For example, SCORE's Learning Center offers tips on:

- hands-on leadership,
- renewing yourself as a leader,
- cultivating confident employees,
- effective leadership,
- exemplary leadership,
- how to create an innovative environment,
- how to empower your employees,
- knowing when you are getting stale,
- teaching employees to "own" their work, and
- what employees want from you as a leader.

SCORE's Web site also offers mentoring resources for veteran, women, and minority managers. Its Reading Room contains many articles on human resources, leadership, and training. Its Sixty Second Guides, which offer advice on how to find a mentor or a coach, are available in both English and Spanish.

BOOKS

Numerous books on the topic of mentoring have been published in recent years. Here are our four favorite books on the general topic of mentoring as well as classics in the various skills areas for managers as mentors.

Mentoring, General

The Mentor's Guide: Facilitating Effective Learning Relationships by Lois J. Zachary (San Francisco: Jossey-Bass), 2000. A comprehensive and accessible review of the complex and sometimes contradictory process of mentoring. Zachary conceptualizes mentoring as a relationship of adult learning and complements this analysis with numerous illustrations, exercises, and suggestions for good practice.

Mentoring: How to Develop Successful Mentor Behaviors by Gordon F. Shea (Menlo Park, California: Crisp Publications), 2002. This book provides the tools to understand the unique role of mentors in today's workplace, determine the most effective mentoring style for your situation, establish agreements to ensure a successful and rewarding relationship, and avoid behaviors that may interfere with mentee growth and development. Mentoring is a rewarding relationship that benefits both participants and the organization. The relationship is now seen as a process of two people working together for mutual gain and enrichment based on their shared experience. Today's mentoring has evolved from simple training of the employee to a productive relationship that offers guidance and counsel to develop another's abilities to the fullest.

Managers as Mentors: Building Partnerships for Learning by Chip R. Bell (San Francisco: Berrett-Koehler), 2002. This book is about power-free facilitation of learning, about teaching through consultation and affection rather than constriction and assessment. It describes learning as an expansive, unfolding process rather than an evaluative, narrowing effort. Most importantly, it is a workbook filled with ideas, suggestions, how-tos, and resources. It was created to serve as a tool for one component of the leader's responsibility—helping another to learn and grow.

A Mentor's Companion by Larry Ambrose (Chicago: Perrone-Ambrose), 1998. This is a practical compendium of action and reflection. Its seven brief chapters are designed to help individuals improve on-the-job performance in collaboration with colleagues, supervisors, senior executives, and peers. Its goal is to be a focused, practical guide into the texture of the mentoring interaction between mentor and mentee. Combining a unique recipe of live dialogues between a mentor and her mentee, with guidelines that glean the key learning from the dialogues, the book teaches the moves the mentor should consider in maximizing the learning possibilities for the mentee. Each dialogue and summary is followed by a third course—menus of questions and statements from which the mentor can sample when preparing a mentoring conversation. The purpose of this book is to distinguish and dramatize the skills of the mentor—those probes, those challenges, those inquiries and provocative questions that will inspire thought, stimulate reflection, tap discovery, and generate a new intelligence in the mentee.

Listening

Listening Leaders: The Ten Golden Rules to Listen, Lead & Succeed by Lyman K. Steil and Richard K. Bommelje (Minneapolis, Minnesota: Beaver's Pond Press), 2004. This book directly connects listening with leadership. Although outstanding leaders are outstanding listeners, most leaders have neglected the development of listening attitudes, skills, and knowledge. Based on more than 50 collective years of work with listening leaders throughout the world, Dr. Steil and Dr. Bommelje have created 10 practical, proven, and priceless rules to enhance everyone's listening and leadership success.

Questioning

Leading with Questions by Michael J. Marquardt (San Francisco: Jossey-Bass), 2005. This book describes how to ask questions with power, the attributes of the questioning leader, when and where leaders should ask questions, the impact of questions on the leader as well as the questioner, the impact questions for the organization and for groups, how questions can transform individuals, and how to become a leader who asks questions.

Smart Questions by Dorothy Leeds (New York: Penguin Putnam), 2000. This is a guide for managers to becoming truly great at getting the most from employees. It shows how to motivate others, turn questions into positive actions, conduct a good hiring interview, reduce mistakes and solve problems, and gain control over volatile situations.

Setting Goals and Expectations

Make Success Measurable! A Mindbook-Workbook for Setting Goals and Taking Action by Douglas K. Smith (San Francisco: Wiley), 1999. Presents a guide designed to emphasize outcomes as opposed to actions in setting goals. Enables individuals or corporations to avoid activity-based goals that can go on indefinitely and to articulate aggressive outcome-based goals that are specific, measurable, achievable, relevant, and time bound

Building Relationships and a Mentoring Environment

Driving Fear out of the Workplace: Creating the High-Trust, High-Performance Organization by Kathleen D. Ryan and Daniel K. Oestreich (San Francisco: Jossey-Bass), 1998. Advances in technology, new employee-employer relations, and the corporate push to optimize intellectual capital have introduced a host of new workplace anxieties that, left unaddressed, can seriously inhibit individual performance and cripple a company's ability to compete. This book discusses how managers can confront the fears that permeate today's organizations so that they can become the high-trust, high-performance organizations of tomorrow. The authors also dig deeply into the root causes of fear and the pervasive "flu of mistrust" that weakens motivation and commitment.

Problem Solving

Solving Tough Problems: An Open Way of Talking, Listening, and Creating New Realities by Adam Kahane (San Francisco: Barrett-Koehler), 2004. The book explores the connection between individual learning and institutional change and how leaders can move beyond politeness and formal statements, beyond routine debate and defensiveness, toward deeper and more productive dialogue. The author explores models, technologies, and examples that foster and facilitate "dialogues of the heart."

Smart Questions: Learn How to Ask the Right Questions for Powerful Results by Gerald Nadler and William Chandon (San Francisco: Jossey-Bass),

2004. This book offers a model and new paradigm for problem solving and creating solutions. It introduces a holistic thinking approach that builds on three foundations—focusing on uniqueness, purposeful information, and systems.

Understanding of and Commitment to Learning

Understanding and Facilitating Adult Learning: A Comprehensive Analysis of Principles and Effective Practices by Stephen D. Brookfield (San Francisco: Jossey-Bass), 1991. A thoroughly researched and extensively documented book efficiently outlines 20 years of studies on adult learning. Effective adult learning practices are explained from six categories: voluntary engagement, respect among participants, collaboration and negotiation of needs, reflective praxis, critical appreciation of diversity, and student empowerment of self-improvement. Aside from the institutional mode of learning, external authority, set objectives, set teaching roles, prescribed evaluation, adult learning seeks to empower self-directed learners with critical thinking modes.

The Adult Learner: The Definitive Classic in Adult Education and Human Resource Development (5th edition) by Malcolm S. Knowles (Houston, Texas: Gulf Publishing), 1998. This book takes you through all of the major educational theories in a clear and no-nonsense style. This book is a very thorough and a terrific primer for anyone interested in learning more about adult and traditional education.

Facilitation

The Skilled Facilitator by Roger Schwarz (San Francisco: Jossey-Bass), 2002. *The Skilled Facilitator* provides essential materials, including simple but effective ground rules for governing group interaction: what to say to a group (and when to say it) to keep it on track and moving toward its goal, proven techniques for starting meetings on the right track (and ending them positively and decisively), practical methods for handling emotions (particularly negative emotions) when they arise in a group context, and a diagnostic approach for helping both facilitators and group members to identify and solve problems that can undermine the group process. The book provides a clearly defined set of basic principles to help facilitators develop sound, value-based responses to a wide range of unpredictable situations. It also includes advice on how to work with outside consultants and facilitate within one's own organization, along with a groundbreaking section on facilitative leadership.

Analytical and Systems Thinking

Systems Thinking: Managing Chaos and Complexity by Jamshid Gharajedaghi (Burlington, Massachusetts: Butterworth-Heinemann), 1999. This book goes beyond the simple declaration of the desirability of systems thinking and provides a practical orientation along with a theoretical depth. It deals operationally with the art of simplifying complexity, managing interdependency, and understanding choice using a novel scheme called iterative design. Twelve chapters discuss systems philosophy, theories, methodology, and practice.

Reflection and Feedback

Feedback Toolkit: 16 Tools for Better Communication in the Workplace by Rick Mauer (Portland, Oregon: Productivity Press), 1994. This book discusses 16 tools for better communication in the workplace. It also defines feedback and tells why effective feedback is important for high performance.

Becoming a Great Manager/Mentor

Managers and mentors develop and improve their skills through action and reflection. They become balanced, open, curious, and courageous, for example, by trying to be these things and by reflecting on their progress. The image of the wise guru on top of the hill can be misleading. The guru did not grow up on top of the hill, but rather through persistence, dedication, action, and reflection developed character, values, and skills. The image of the hill signifies that the guru is now dwelling in the results of lifelong efforts and is able to be a resource to others.

Serving as a mentor is one of the most important and valuable services that a manager can provide to a colleague. We hope we have provided the reader with the principles and practices as well as the resources to become an effective mentor.

Notes

Chapter 1

1. Stone, F. (2004). *Mentoring as a leadership development strategy.* American Management Association, AMA Online Library. Retrieved July 7, 2004, from http://www.amanet.org/online_library/bestofMO/lead/02_DevLeadStrategy.cfm

2. Kerka, S. (1998). New perspectives on mentoring. *ERIC Digest, 194.* Retrieved September 9, 2004, from http://www.ericdigests.org/1998-3/mentoring.html

3. *Definitions of mentoring.* (2002). National Mentoring Network. Retrieved June 11, 2004, from http://mandbf.org.uk/mentoring_and_befriending/25.

4. Kreisler, H. (2001). Conversation with James O. Freedman. Institute of International Studies, UC Berkeley. Retrieved November 4, 2004, from http://globetrotter.berkeley.edu/people/Freedman/freedman-con3.html

5. Clutterbuck, D. (2004). Making the most of informal mentoring: A positive climate is key. Development and Learning in Organizations, 18(4), 16–17.

6. Thompson, S. (2000, March). *Next wave eCommunication: New rules, new roles in communication leadership.* IABC Conference, Washington, D.C. Retrieved August 4, 2004, from http://www.fcn.gov/reinvent/pool/press45.htm

7. Fujie, H. J., & Johnson, C. S. (2000). *A cross-cultural perspective on cross-cultural mentoring.* American Bar Association, Commission of Racial and Ethnic Diversity in the Profession, Goal IX, 6(3). Retrieved July 2, 2004, from http://www.abanet.org/minorities/publications/g9/v6n3/fujiejohnson.html

8. McElroy, M. (2003). *The new knowledge management: Complexity, learning and sustainable innovation*, p. 151. Amsterdam: Butterworth-Heinemann.

9. Zachary, L. J. (2000). *The mentors guide: Facilitating effective learning relationships*, p. 3. San Francisco: Jossey-Bass.

10. DeVoto, E. (Ed.). (1997). *The journals of Lewis and Clark.* Boston: Mariner Books.

11. Zuboff, S. (1988). *In the age of the smart machine: The future of work and power*, p. 395. Oxford: Heinemann.

12. Van Buren. (2001). *State of the Industry Report 2001.* Alexandria, VA: ASTD Press, 1.

13. Marquardt, M. (1999). *The Global Advantage: How to Improve Performance through Globalization.* Houston: Gulf Press.

14. Wong, P.T.P. (1999). A mentoring approach to management education. International Network on Personal Meaning. Retrieved June 18, 2004, from http://www.meaning.ca/articles/mentoring_management.html

15. Goldsworthy, A. (2000). *The heart and soul of leadership: Leadership in the networked world.* Spring Hill: Australian Institute of Management.

16. Manuzon, M. T. (2001). Managing foreigners. *Philippine Business Magazine, 8*(2). Retrieved August 8, 2004, from http://www.philippinebusiness.com.ph/archives/magazine/vol8-2001/8-2/cover story.htm

17. Mayor, T. (2001). *Learning to supervise remote workers.* IT World.com. Retrieved August 4, 2005 from http://www.itworld.com/Career/4109/CIO010401remote/

18. Byrne, J., Brandt, R., and Port, O. *The virtual corporation.* Business Week online, February 8, 1993. Retrieved July 26, 2005 from http://www.businessweek.com/@@J1JaMouQtnJSthEA/archives/1993/b330454.arc.htm

19. Owen, H. (1991). *Riding the tiger: Doing business in a transforming world.* Potomac, MD: Abbott, 1.

20. Revans, R. (1983). *The ABCs of Action Learning.* Bromley, England: Chartwell Brat., 11.

21. Drucker, P. F. (1999). *The new commandments of change.* Inc Magazine, June 1999. Retrieved August 4, 2005 from http://www.inc.com/magazine/19990601/804.html.

22. Stewart, T.A. (1991). Brainpower. *Fortune* (June 3), p. 44.

23. Wriston, W. (1992). *The twilight of sovereignty: How the information revolution is transforming the world,* p. 8. New York: Scribner.

24. Stacey, R.D. (1992). *Managing the unknowable: Strategic boundaries between order and chaos in organizations.* San Francisco: Jossey-Bass.

25. Managers Forum. (2004). eLearning: Statistics. Retrieved September 9, 2004, from http://www.managersforum.com/eLearning/Statistics.htm

26. Goldsworthy, A. (2000). *The heart and soul of leadership: Leadership in the networked world.* Spring Hill: Australian Institute of Management.

27. Phillips-Jones, L. (2003). Mentoring is crucial in these economic times. *Church Business* (July 2003). Retrieved June 16, 2004, from http://www.churchbusiness.com/articles/371cover1.html

28. Howard Rice Nemerovski Canady Falk & Rabin. (2004). Associate Training and Mentoring. Retrieved August 1, 2005 from http://www.howardrice.com/content.contentDetail&id=7686&lid=0

29. Smith, G.P. (2003). The importance of having a good mentor. *Chart Your Course International.* Retrieved July 16, 2004, from http://www.chartcourse.com/articlementor.html

30. Bell, C. (2002). *Managers as mentors: Building partnerships for learning,* p. xxi. San Francisco: Berrett-Koehler.

31. Kelly, D. (2003). *Organized group mentoring & achievement: A study of high achieving Black adults.* African American Success Foundation. Retrieved July 6, 2004, from http://www.blacksuccessfoundation.org/sci_report_abstract-group_mentoring.htm

32. Cleaver, J., & Spence, B. (2004). All the right stuff: NAFE's top 30 companies for executive women. NAFE. Retrieved August 8, 2004, from http://nafe.com/top30_03.shtml

33. Mentoring: The path to success? (2002). YourPeopleManager.com. Retrieved June 6, 2004, from http://www.yourpeoplemanager.com/YRqieONoivVsHw.html

34. Engstrøm, T. (2003). Can we share tacit knowledge through mentoring? (abstract). *Peer Resources.* Retrieved August 4, 2005 from http://www.mentors.ca.thementornews07.htmlRE:

35. Wedin, R. (2003). The meaning of mentoring. *Today's Chemist at Work, 12*(3), 41–41.

36. Ibid.

37. Rick, C. (2003). Statement before the House Committee on Veterans Affairs (October 2, 2003). Retrieved September 6, 2004, from http://www.va.gov/OCA/testimony/031002CR_usa.htm

38. Phillips-Jones, L. (2003). Mentoring is crucial in these economic times. *Church Business* (July 2003). Retrieved June 16, 2004, from http://www.churchbusiness.com/articles/371cover1.html

39. Janas, M. (1996). Mentoring the mentor: A challenge for staff development. *Journal of Staff Development, 17*(4), 2–5.

40. Managers Forum. (2004). eLearning: Statistics. Retrieved September 9, 2004, from http://www.managersforum.com/eLearning/Statistics.htm

41. Kerka, S. (1998). New perspectives on mentoring. *ERIC Digest, 194.* Retrieved September 9, 2004, from http://www.ericdigests.org/1998-3/mentoring.html

42. Virtual Advisor, Inc. (2002). Managing employees in a global marketplace. VA Interactive. Retrieved August 1, 2005, from http://www.va-interactive.com/inbusiness/editorial/hr/articles/managing.html

43. Ibid.

44. Phillips, S. (2004). *Can humility, faith be good for business? Business management model catching on with companies.* MSNBC News (February 28, 2004). Retrieved August 1, 2005, from http://msnbc.msn.com/id/4374722/

45. Jacobs, J.A., and Gerson, K. (2004). *The time divide: Work, family, and gender inequality.* Cambridge: Harvard University Press.

46. Martin, C. (2004). Talent drain. *Darwin Magazine* (June 2004). Retrieved August 9, 2004, from http://www.darwinmag.com/read/060104/talent.html

47. Janas, M. (1996). Mentoring the mentor: A challenge for staff development. *Journal of Staff Development, 17*(4), 2–5.

48. Gray, W., & Gray, M. (1985). Synthesis of research mentoring beginning teachers. *Educational Leadership, 43*(3), 37–43.

49. Thies-Sprinthall, L. (1986). A collaborative approach for mentor training: A working model. *Journal of Teacher Education, 37*(6), 13–20.

50. Clutterbuck, D. (2004). Making the most of informal mentoring: A positive climate is key. Development and Learning in Organizations, 18(4), 16–17.

Chapter 2

1. Walker, J. T., & Lofton, S. P. (2003). Effect of a problem based learning curriculum on students' perceptions of self directed learning. *Issues in Educational Research, 13,* 71–100.

2. Kerka, S. (1998). New perspectives on mentoring. *ERIC Digest, 194.* Retrieved September 9, 2004, from http://www.ericdigests.org/1998-3/mentoring.html

3. Clutterbuck, D. (2004). Making the most of informal mentoring: A positive climate is key. Development and Learning in Organizations, 18(4), 16–17.

4. Flannes, S. W., & Levin, G. (2001). *People skills for project managers.* Vienna, VA: Management Concepts.

5. Hansen, C. (2000).Virtual mentoring: A real-world case study. Graduate paper, Educational Communications and Technology, University of Saskatchewan. Retrieved July 23, 2004, from http://www.usask.ca/education/coursework/802papers/hansen/hansen.htm

6. El-Shinnawy, M., & Markus, M. (1997). The poverty of media richness theory: Explaining people's choice of electronic mail versus voice mail. *International Journal of Human Computer Studies, 46,* 443–467.

7. Brinson, J., & Kotler, J. (1993). Cross-cultural mentoring in counselor education: A strategy for retaining minority faculty. *Counselor Education and Supervision, x,* 241–253.

Watts, R. (1987). Development of professional identity in Black clinical psychology students. *Professional Psychology: Research and Practice, 18,* 28–35.

8. General Mills Web site. Retrieved August 1, 2005 from: http://www.generalmills.com/corporate/commitment/workforce.aspx

9. Minor, T. (n.d.). Mentors lead the way to success. BET.com. Retrieved July 7, 2004, from http://diversity.bet.monster.com/afam/articles/mentoring/

10. Zachary, L. (2000). *The mentors guide,* pp. 38–42. San Francisco: Jossey-Bass.

11. Marquardt, M. (2004). *Optimizing the power of action learning: Solving problems and building leaders in real time.* Palo Alto, CA: Davies-Black.

12. Wenger, E. (1998). Communities of practice: Learning as a social system. Community Intelligence Labs Web page. Retrieved August 1, 2005 from: http://www.co-i-l.com./coil/knowledge-garden/cop/lss.shtml

13. The National Environmental Education and Training Foundation Institute for Corporate Environmental Mentoring (ICEM). Environmental mentoring: Benefits, challenges, and opportunities. Retrieved August 1, 2005 from: http://www.neetf.org/pubs/envmentorbco.pdf

14. Kerka, S. (1998). New perspectives on mentoring. *ERIC Digest, 194.* Retrieved September 9, 2004, from http://www.ericdigests.org/1998-3/mentoring.html

15. Galvin, T. (2002). The 2002 top 100. Training, *39*(3), 20–68.

16. Maher, K. (2004, May 31). Reverse mentoring: Executives pump junior staff for the wisdom of youth. *Globe and Mail,* B18.

17. Bell, C. (1997). The bluebird's secret: Mentoring with bravery and balance. *Training and Development, 51*(2), 30–33.

18. Cleminson, A., & Bradford, S. (1996). Professional education. *Journal of Vocational Education and Training, 48*(3), 249–259.

19. Haley, F., & Canabou, C. (2003). The mentor's mentors. *Fast Company, 75*(59). Retrieved July 21, 2004, from http://www.fastcompany.com/magazine/75/fasttalk.html

20. Flannes, S.W., and Levin, G. (2001). *People skills for project mangers.* Vienna, VA: Management Concepts.

21. Ambrose, L. (1998). *A mentor's companion.* Chicago: Perrone-Ambrose.

22. Zachary, L. (2000). *The mentors guide,* p. 73–74. San Francisco: Jossey-Bass.

23. Gilbert, L.A. (1985). Dimensions of same-gender student-faculty role-model relationships. *Sex Roles, 12,* 111–123.

24. Noe, R. (1988). An investigation of the determinants of successful assigned mentoring relationships. *Personnel Psychology, 41,* 457–479.

Rose, G. (1999). What do doctoral students want in a mentor? Development of the ideal mentor scale. *Dissertation Abstracts International, 60*(12B), 6418.

Wilde, J., & Schau, C. (1991). Mentoring in graduate schools of education: Mentees' perceptions. *Journal of Experimental Education, 59,* 165–179.

25. Boreen, J., & Niday, D. (2003). *Mentoring across boundaries: Helping beginning teachers succeed in challenging situations.* Portland, ME: Stenhouse.

Hildred, S. (2002). Project for Aboriginal mMentors—Report. Royal Australian College of General Practitioners. Retrieved August 9, 2004, from http://www.racgp.org.au/downloads/pdf/20030115wafinalreport.pdf

26. Smith, G.P. (2003). The importance of having a good mentor. Chart Your Course International. Retrieved July 16, 2004, from http://www.chartcourse.com/articlementor.html

Chapter 3

1. Ambrose, L. (1998). *A mentor's companion,* p. 6. Chicago: Perrone-Ambrose.

2. Madigan, C. (2000). *It's not your father's mentoring program.* Business Finance Mag.com. Retrieved August 3, 2005 from: http://www.businessfinancemag.com/magazine/archives/article.html?articleID=13661&pg=1

3. Maister, D. (2001). *Practice what you preach: What managers must do to create a high-achievement culture.* New York: Free Press.

4. Seldin, N. (2001). Skillful management. *APS Healthcare, 1*(1). Retrieved August 18, 2004, from http://www.washington.edu/admin/hr/worklife/carelink/nwsltrs/sklfl_mgmt_prac.pdf

5. Goleman, D., McKee, A., & Boyatzis, R. (2002). *Primal leadership: Realizing the power of emotional intelligence.* Cambridge, MA: Harvard Business School Press.

6. Marquardt, M. (2004). *Optimizing the power of action learning: Solving problems and building leaders in real time.* Palo Alto, CA: Davies-Black.

7. Strong, B. (2001). *Create creative mood at work.* Deseret News Archives, Sunday April 15, 2001. Retrieved August 3, 2005 from: http://marriottschool.byu.edu/cfe/resources/DeseretNews/dno4_15_01.html

8. Ambrose, L. (1998). *A mentor's companion,* p. 13. Chicago: Perrone-Ambrose.

9. Ibid., p. 38.

10. Zachary, L. (2000). *The mentors guide,* p. 49. San Francisco: Jossey-Bass.

11. Ibid., p. 50.

12. Ambrose, L. (1998). *A mentor's companion,* p. 21–22. Chicago: Perrone-Ambrose.

13. Zachary, L. (2000). *The mentors guide,* p. 61. San Francisco: Jossey-Bass.

14. Ibid., p. 51.

15. Ambrose, L. (1998). *A mentor's companion,* p. 23. Chicago: Perrone-Ambrose.

16. Zachary, L. (2000). *The mentors guide,* p. 52. San Francisco: Jossey-Bass.

17. Ambrose, L. (1998). *A mentor's companion,* p. 8. Chicago: Perrone-Ambrose.

18. Zachary, L. (2000). *The mentors guide,* p. 141. San Francisco: Jossey-Bass.

19. Ambrose, L. (1998). *A mentor's companion,* p. 37. Chicago: Perrone-Ambrose.

20. Ibid., p. 12–13.

21. Ibid., p. 51–52.

22. Zachary, L. (2000). *The mentors guide,* p. 149. San Francisco: Jossey-Bass.

23. Ibid., p. 151.

24. Clutterbuck, D. (2002). Why mentoring programmes and relationships fail. Link&Learn eNewsletter (archives). Retrieved August 3, 2005 from: http://www.linkageinc.com/company/news_events/link_learn_enewsletter/archive/2002/12_02_mentoring_clutterbuck.aspx

25. Ibid.

Chapter 4

1. Autry, J. (1991). *Love and profit: The art of caring leadership.* New York: William Morrow and Company.

2. Shea, G. F. (2002). *Mentoring,* p. 33. Menlo Park, NJ: Crisp.

3. Roberts, W. (1988). *The enculturation of battlefield leaders for the twenty-first century.* The Omar N. Bradley Lecture Series address presented at the U.S. Army Command General Staff College, Leavenworth, Kansas.

4. Zachary, L. (2000). *The mentors guide,* p. 19. San Francisco: Jossey-Bass.

5. Kofman, F. & Senge, P. (1995). Communities of commitment: The heart of learning organizations, in *Learning Organizations*, eds. S. Chawla & J. Renesch. Oregon: Productivity Press, p. 38.

6. Seldin, N. (2001). Skillful management. *APS Healthcare, 1*(1). Retrieved August 18, 2004, from http://www.washington.edu/admin/hr/worklife/carelink/nwsltrs/sklfl_mgmt_prac.pdf, p. 2.

7. Shea, G. F. (2002). *Mentoring*, p. 67. Menlo Park, NJ: Crisp.

8. Ibid., p. 35.

9. Bell, C. (2002). *Managers as mentors: Building partnerships for learning*, p. 110. San Francisco: Berrett-Koehler.

10. Zachary, L. (2000). *The mentors guide*, p. 162. San Francisco: Jossey-Bass.

11. Ibid., pp. 53–56.

Chapter 5

1. Shea, G. F. (2002). *Mentoring*, p. 24. Menlo Park, NJ: Crisp.

Chapter 6

1. Phillips-Jones, L. (2003). Mentoring is crucial in these economic times. *Church Business* (July 2003). Retrieved June 16, 2004, from http://www.churchbusiness.com/articles/371cover1.html

Chapter 7

1. Goldberg, M. (1998). *The art of the question: A guide to short-term question-centered therapy.* New York: John Wiley.

2. Ibid.

3. Ibid.

4. Ibid.

Index

About the Authors

MICHAEL J. MARQUARDT is Professor of Human Resources Development and Program Director of Overseas Programs at George Washington University. A consultant and training specialist, he is also President of Global Learning Associates and Director of the Global Institute of Action Learning. He is an award-winning author of numerous books, including *Building the Learning Organization* (Academy of HRD book of the year). *Action Learning in Action, Global Teams* and, with Peter Loan, *HRD in the Age of Globalization.*

PETER LOAN is a director and principal consultant of Brown and Loan Associates, specializing in management and cross-cultural training. He is the author, with Michael J. Marquardt, of *HRD in the Age of Globalization.*